AMERICA'S STAKE IN ASIA

For Tap
who know far
more about it
than I.

Theron

New York
24/3/68

Books by Drew Middleton

AMERICA'S STAKE IN ASIA

Drew Middleton

J. B. LIPPINCOTT COMPANY
Philadelphia & New York

To P.S.P. and E.L.P.

Introduction

When I set out for Asia early in 1967, I had no intention of writing a book. I went to learn what I could about countries of which I knew little. My knowledge was limited to what I had heard and read in a quarter of a century of international reporting. I had few prejudices.

I visited thirteen countries and the British Crown Colony of Hong Kong. As the journey progressed I began to realize that the situation in these countries and the comments of their people differed sharply from what I had been led to expect. To mention only one point: I did not find that the United States intervention in South Vietnam was resented. On the contrary, it was regarded, except by the Communists and their clients, as a shield.

We are engaged in a great struggle in Asia extending from Japan to Iran. Prolonged quarrels about why we are so engaged are not as important as ensuring that the struggle goes our way and that the people, the hundreds of millions of people, who are dependent on the United States are not sacrificed to our irresolution and blindness.

To show what Americans are doing in Asia, what the Asians themselves are doing, and to give some picture of the problems that plague the continent are the purposes of this book. The opinions, of course, are my own. I am happy to say they bear no relation to those of the editorial page of *The New York Times*.

DREW MIDDLETON

Westport
New York
August-October 1967

Contents

I

The Challenge to Asia

One hot evening I sat and talked with Prince Souvanna Phouma, the Premier and Foreign Minister of Laos. It was a somber discussion, as any talk of Laos must be, for Laos is in the front line of the struggle in Southeast Asia against North Vietnam and communism. But in the last six months there had been more successes than defeats for the Prince's forces, and as we neared the end of our talk his face brightened.

"And this year we will plant perhaps fifteen thousand more hectares of rice," he said happily.

By such basic values must the great struggle for Southeast Asia be judged. As I walked back to the hotel through the dusty streets of Vientiane, the little administrative capital of Laos, I thought what those fifteen thousand hectares could mean: food for families, a small profit at harvest time, hope that next year the Vietnamese and the Pathet Lao, the military arm of the Laotian Communist Party, would have been forced to yield still more paddy for rice.

The fighting in northern and eastern Laos represents one small part of the continuing struggle for the future of Southeast Asia. In one sense this struggle is a race between communism and the free states that lie south of China. Can these states develop political stability and economic viability and group themselves in regional organizations before Communist China establishes political hegemony and economic domination over that part of the world?

The issue is now in the balance. The struggle nears its climax. From the busy, noisy streets of Tokyo westward across Asia to where the white-topped wall of the Himalayas frowns down on the Indian plains, it occupies the thoughts and energies of

11

hundreds of millions of people. The struggle takes many forms. In Vietnam it is a desperate war. In Malaysia it is an intensive effort to bring the smiling, placid people of the forest into this century. In Indonesia society is being rebuilt on an indigenous basis, now that the Communists have been ousted. In India the fight begins—and quite possibly will be decided—in the fields and rice paddies, for unless the Indians can feed themselves and establish a viable economy they may sink into either foreign vassalage or internal disruption.

The struggle has not been lost. It certainly will be lost if the United States listens to those who demand disengagement in Asia, the withdrawal of American forces from Vietnam, and an end to political, military, and economic commitments elsewhere in the area. To do so would sentence some hundreds of thousands of our friends and allies to death and imprisonment, commit unnumbered millions to life under communism, and weaken faith in our word among anxious allies elsewhere in the world.

Southeast Asia is the focus of a world struggle. If the free nations there win, with American help, in the sense that they purchase time to build political institutions and economic well-being, then the nature of the struggle will change and the contest with communism may well enter a less explosive phase. If Southeast Asia falls, any of half a dozen states may be communism's next target. Bad as South Vietnam is, it is infinitely better than the war America may be forced to fight if Southeast Asia falls.

Such sentiments are not novel. I put them forward only because fourteen weeks of travel from Tokyo to Teheran convinced me of their validity. I began my travels convinced that many opportunities had been lost to make peace in Vietnam. I was highly dubious about the wisdom of the American effort there. At the end I felt, with some bitterness, that, although chances for peacemaking had been missed, this was now irrelevant. We were engaged, and withdrawal would create more difficulties for the United States and more grief for ourselves, our allies, and our friends than remaining and fighting it out. These are not easy thoughts to lie awake with in the hot Asian nights.

Southeast Asia faces two challenges to its political independence and economic stability. The first, most evident and currently most dangerous, is that posed by North Vietnamese military aggression. I do not specify Communist aggression, although North Vietnam is a Communist state, because that is not the way people in Vietnam or Laos or Thailand, the countries now principally engaged, see the problem. Their attitude toward the North Vietnamese reminded me strongly of that of western European peoples toward the Germans thirty years ago. They regarded them as aggressors pure and simple. They had no doubt that the North Vietnamese had instigated and encouraged the Viet Cong insurrection in South Vietnam and then, when they overestimated their chances of victory, had moved in their main army to defeat the South Vietnamese and the Americans. They knew that North Vietnamese regulars supported the Communist Pathet Lao in Laos and, on their own, had claimed and occupied sizable parts of the eastern and northern provinces of that country. They knew that the North Vietnamese had inspired, armed, and supported the insurrection against the Thai Government in northern Vietnam.

So in Southeast Asia, and even in India and Burma, I heard very few demands to "stop the bombing" by the United States Air Force of North Vietnam. Nor did I hear—except, naturally, from Communists—any opposition to expansion of the American military effort. The American visitor will hear more of this sort of talk in elegant drawing rooms in London and Paris and in the air-conditioned offices of the United Nations Secretariat, where everyone is oh, so objective against the United States, than he will in hot, dusty villages living under constant fear of North Vietnamese aggression.

13

AMERICA'S STAKE IN ASIA

The second challenge, less immediately evident but ultimately more dangerous, is that posed by Communist China. I have not concluded that Peking now aims at physical conquest of the independent states of South and Southeast Asia. But I believe that she does aim at establishing communism there, through Wars of National Liberation or internal subversion, and to gather this great, rich region into the Chinese economy. For reasons we can examine later, this challenge is not now being pressed as strongly as seemed likely three or four years ago. But no one in authority in the governments concerned doubts it will come and that, through their own energies and American help, they must be prepared to meet it and hold it in check.

As one economics minister said wearily, "Getting our people on their feet doesn't guarantee that the Chinese won't try. But it does guarantee that it will make it harder for them to succeed."

These are the dimensions of the struggle. No one can, or should, pretend that our friends and allies are stainless crusaders, high-mindedly devoted to all the ideals Americans cherish. There are knaves and traitors. This is Asia, where corruption and nepotism are part of life. Faced with the imminent fear of death at the hands of the Vietnamese or tired by the long, sometimes seemingly fruitless effort to establish a balance to China, men will defect, will sell secrets. If America cannot approve of this, she must become accustomed to it.

And in the end, there will be no victory as most Americans understand it; only, with luck, five or ten years of comparative stability in which South and Southeast Asia can build for a peaceful future.

The struggle has not been lost. Indeed it seemed that in many battlefields—and battlefields may be rice paddies devoted to the culture of new, richer rice strains as well as the hot, clamorous clearings of battalion headquarters in Vietnam—the United States and its friends and allies were more than holding our own.

We can look at the causes for encouragement later in detail, seeing how each affects different countries. The first is the concentration by the Communist Chinese on their own internal differences, expressed in what in Peking is called the Cultural Revolution. Come to think of it, this is an odd name. For as it develops, rolling through the cities and across the farmlands of China, it is more a civil war than a revolution. And it certainly is not cultural.

This revolution, civil war, ideological dispute, call it what you will, has promoted the second cause. This is a perceptible movement away from support of Communist China on the part of the overseas Chinese. There may be as many as 15 million of them, from Manila to Burma, and the name for them in Chinese, Hwa Ch'iao, "the sojourners," is apt. They formed— and may form again in the future—an overseas community that gave economic help and political loyalty to the Communists. For, whether they were Communists or not themselves, they saw in the China of Mao Tse-tung the revival of a national dream of a united, powerful China, an entity that would be respected in the world.

For them the spread of the Cultural Revolution means the abandonment, perhaps temporary, perhaps final, of their hopes. These "sojourners" are turning then to the lands where they work and, in many cases, have grown wealthy, as their true homes.

Another cause is the check to North Vietnamese aggression administered by the American and allied forces in Vietnam. No one pretended that this was the end. No one saw it as more than a check. But for the first time something had been done to halt the aggressor that defeated the French, started insurrection in

Laos and Thailand, and defied the Americans in Vietnam. For the time being the pressure was eased. There was time to breathe.

Finally, Indonesia. President Sukarno was moving into retirement, the Communists had been massacred, the pro-Communist Chinese evicted. The nightmare of an organized, potent Communist state lying in the sea facing Southern Asia from the Philippines to Malaysia was gone. Here the lesson was simple. Communism is not inevitable. Communists can be defeated. This is simple but very important to peoples whose religions, whose harsh lives, teach resignation.

The Asian political struggle, as we shall see, is accompanied by another, the fight for food. Here again, it takes on the character of a race between the growing demands for food, principally rice, and the efforts to increase the production of food. The two struggles are interwoven. Rice is as much ammunition as mortar bombs. The trebled production of rice in the village of Kadda in East Pakistan may mean as much, ultimately, to the outcome of the struggle as the elimination of a guerrilla chief in northern Thailand.

The popular vision of Southeast Asia as an economic slum is a false one. This area, from Mindanao's nickel to Afghanistan's iron ore, is rich in resources. If population control works—and this is a very large "if"—the area can feed itself, it can produce a greater volume of raw materials, and the rate at which living standards are rising throughout free Asia will be accelerated.

Great problems, massive difficulties, lie ahead. But everywhere I saw a noticeable sense of determination on the part of Asians: bright young men in offices in Bangkok, Manila, and Rawalpindi, farmers in the back country of Luzon and along the Mekong in Laos. They believed, emphatically that their countries, and Asia, could increase food production, could exploit its natural resources, and eventually would emerge from this turbulent era richer and stronger than ever before in history.

In 1966 I visited most of the states of sub-Saharan Africa. There I had found societies that in many cases included areas and peoples just emerging from primitive tribalism. There was a profound difference in Asia. Here were peoples with cultures and histories, quicker to accept the benefits of modern technology. The rice farmer in Thailand who finds that a new strain of rice increases his yearly production and, as a result, moves from subsistence agriculture to sales of his surplus is the true revolutionary in Asia. For he is slowly generating the demand for consumer goods and, at the same time, helping to meet the demand for food.

Asians are willing to accept foreign aid. They understand that they need help in many fields. But they are not content, as so many charge, to sit back and rely on it alone. Asians work hard, incredibly hard when the climate and their diet are considered. Nor have Communist efforts to convince Asians that western aid and western investment lead to "neocolonialism" succeeded. There was far less anti-Americanism, far more gratitude for American help, than I had anticipated.

The views I heard on this and other subjects came from politicians, government officials, foreign diplomats, bankers, shopkeepers, businessmen, farmers, and chance acquaintances met on planes and buses and in restaurants. Below that level people either have no knowledge of the society in which they live and the world beyond or, when they do, are too occupied by the unending struggle for food, for life itself, to think about problems other than their own.

Any discussion of Asian public opinion must include the caveat that informed public opinion, as we know it in the West, is relatively small, although, even so, it is much larger than in black Africa. It is unrealistic to talk of Asia or even an Asian country being "against" the war in Vietnam or "outraged" by

American bombing there. A very small percentage of the people hold any ideas at all on such subjects, and an even smaller percentage expresses its ideas.

I asked an American diplomat at a luncheon what he regarded as the approximate size of informed public opinion in India. His estimate of 10 per cent was corrected by the Indian on my right. He put it at "no more than five per cent, perhaps not that"; in other words, 26 million people out of India's estimated 520 million.

"And don't forget," the Indian added, "that we who are educated and literate have different habits of thought, different backgrounds, than the millions you see around you. We're brown Englishmen. There is a gap between we and 'they.' We're trying to bridge it, but it will take many years."

My conclusion was that a remarkably large part of informed public opinion in the countries I visited either openly or tacitly approves the United States involvement in Vietnam. The majority of these states, allied or neutral, are vulnerable to Communist pressure either from the Vietnamese or from the Chinese. Mao Tse-tung and Marshal Lin Piao in their glorification of Wars of National Liberation have told the independent Asian governments how they intend to overthrow them. Consequently when the Americans intervened to stop the overthrow of an independent government in a war that, although inspired and fought by the North Vietnamese, followed the Chinese pattern, hope and confidence increased.

This did not mean, of course, that Asians liked Americans any more or any less or that they accepted American values. It did mean they recognized that someone was doing something about North Vietnamese aggression, something that might give the Chinese pause, and they were grateful.

Many Asians, especially the Japanese, had feared in 1965, when the Johnson Administration raised the military stakes in Vietnam, that this would provoke Chinese military intervention. When this did not develop and when the tide of war began to run perceptibly against the North Vietnamese, support for the United States increased, reflecting a tendency, human enough, to side with the stronger power.

Much has been made by the Communists and their allies of the supposed American intention to remain in Asia. Instead of concern on this point, I found, from Manila around to Kuala Lumpur, anxiety lest the Americans, wearied by a long and expensive war, cut their commitments and leave the peoples of the area to the Chinese and their allies. Asian politicians ordinarily do not make speeches about it, but they are very conscious of the importance of American nuclear protection as a safeguard to Chinese pressure or outright aggression.

"We want to make our own future," Narciso Ramos, the Philippine Foreign Minister said, "but we want you on the sidelines to make sure we make it ourselves without interruption from our 'friends' up north."

The American involvement in Asia, of course, is much wider than the military operations in Vietnam and Thailand. The technical assistance being given Asians in agriculture, water control, public health, and many other fields is widely appreciated. I had many occasions to feel proud I was an American in Asia, but never more so than when I saw the work being done by patient, dedicated, enthusiastic Americans. The best example I encountered is the International Rice Research Institute at Los Baños in the Philippines. Financed by the Ford and Rockefeller Foundations, the institute has succeeded in developing a strain of rice known as IR-8.

With reasonable care IR-8 can at least double rice production in wide areas of Asia. In some areas production has been trebled. Think of what this means to a continent struggling to banish the age-old specter of famine!

Even in the middle of harangues about the unwisdom of American policy in Vietnam, Indian intellectuals would interject thanks for the wheat and rice shipped to their country to feed its ill-nourished millions. A burly Afghan truck driver stared at me in a restaurant, then got up, walked over, and put his hand on my shoulder.

"Americans make good roads," he said.

The American image in Asia, then, is a much brighter one than our enemies would have us believe. The underlying reason is that Asians understand, as many Americans and most Europeans do not, the nature of the military and political danger and the necessity for outside help if they are to build stable economies.

Southeast Asia is not lost. It can only be lost by an American withdrawal in both the military and the air fields. To withdraw now would invite as many dangers for us and for the Asians in the future as did the return to isolationism in the twenties. This Asia, the sun-baked plains, the steaming jungles, the teeming cities, is part of the same world, one that the jets bring closer to America every day.

Southeast Asia can be made into a stable area, strong enough to resist communism in the future. To do so will require a combination of Asian energy and American help coupled to far-sighted United States diplomacy. Present and future American administrations must do their utmost to promote regionalism in Southeast Asia and to bring the two great states on the area's flanks, Japan and India, into cooperation with any groupings evolved by the states of Southeast Asia. This is the dream of many in Asia now.

In this struggle for the future of Southeast and South Asia there will be no great national triumphs for the United States. Just as there are no battle maps demonstrating American and allied military progress in South Vietnam—it is not that sort of war—so there can be no maps or charts or tables that accurately show the ebb and flow of the larger economic and political struggle. Americans should forget the tendency to compare the Vietnam war or the struggles in Laos and Thailand with World War II. Equally it would be unrealistic to think of the political and economic effort in the area in terms of Marshall Plan help to Europe.

Progress will be slow, in many cases almost imperceptible. It will be represented in the end by small, simple things such as the increase in rice production in a backward province, the election of a village mayor without interruption by the Communists, the laying of a sewer or the installation by a Punjabi farmer of a water pump. The struggle itself is vast, touching every human activity. But the measurement of success must concentrate on the most insignificant aspects of that activity.

In South and Southeast Asia the United States is dealing with possibly the most important segment of the third world, the world of undeveloped and underdeveloped countries. Failure to deal honorably and justly with its peoples will increase the prospects of failure elsewhere. The struggle on which the United States and the independent people of this area are embarked cannot be dismissed as the wrong war, at the wrong place, at the wrong time, either in its military or its political, economic, and social aspects. Americans, soldiers and doctors, agronomists and teachers, *are* in Asia. It is too late to turn back now.

The involvement is and will continue to be costly in men, money, and matériel. Americans will be dealing with folk more alien to our political beliefs and culture than those of Europe. Continued opposition is natural and healthy. But opponents must consider the alternative. What happens to our allies, to our friends, and, ultimately, to America and the world if this vast, rich area drifts under Communist domination?

II

Power, Opportunity, and Caution in Japan

No Westerner ever is really prepared for Tokyo. After the long, quiet flight over the Pacific wastes, the frenzied activity catches him unprepared. People—hundreds, thousands—swarm across the street crossings. Cars, taxis, trolley buses sweep in swift phalanxes down the avenues; others dart out of dim side streets. Lights flash, electric signs wink, horns blare, a train rushes past on an elevated track. It is noisier than Chicago, more hectic than New York, a thousand times more "swinging" than London. Is it all aimless, activity seeking only the false sense of security that activity gives? There is no impression of orderly power as there is in Washington today and as there was in London a generation ago.

Yet Tokyo is both the focus and the expression of an authentic miracle of national revival. The government rules 100 million people: virile, industrious, and capable. Here on these islands on the eastern edge of Asia is a country whose capacity for good or ill in Asia is almost incalculable. Japan can be the pillar and prop of political and economic cooperation as far west as Burma. Or Japan can use its financial and industrial power solely for her own ends, expanding the trade connection with China and the Soviet Union, gradually rebuilding her military strength, and, finally, venturing into the military uses of atomic energy.

In Washington diplomats think in terms of "our" Japan, a country that will further American policy in Southeast Asia by contributing to its economic development and by becoming the American-inspired mainspring of regional groupings on the basis of which international political stability for the area can be developed.

In Tokyo it is quite apparent that those who direct and control this furious energy see their opportunities, but they have not yet decided the course Japan is to follow. In all probability the decision will be made within the next year and a half; in Japan's present psychological condition it is most unlikely that the decision will be signaled to the world. The fundamental impression is one of wariness.

"The Japanese are preparing themselves psychologically for a leadership role in Asia," a western ambassador said. This judgment, shared by many foreigners in the country, is invariably accompanied by the advice that it is useless to look for evidence of this preparation because it is taking place silently, almost by a process of osmosis, in the Establishment.

The Japanese Establishment is the answer to the question that puzzles every visitor. How is this seemingly aimless energy controlled and directed? This is an Establishment older, more coherent, less visible than that in Britain. But its ramifications are wider, its discipline more absolute.

The term "Establishment" was first used in eighteenth-century Britain to define the grouping of political, religious, and governmental interests that was devoted to maintaining the state and the established church as they were. Reintroduced in the fifties of this century, the term was expanded to include all those established organizations, from the Church of England's highest bishops to the heads of the Trades Union Congress, who, to critics, appeared equally adamant against change.

Such an Establishment does exist in Britain. But compared with that of Japan it is a ramshackle affair. Japan's, building for two thousand years, is unique in Asia. It gives the Japanese an immense advantage over old but disorganized societies like

India's and over newer, unstable societies in Southeast Asia.

The key to the strength of the Japanese Establishment is interchangeability. There is a ceaseless flow of able men from the bureaucracy into big business, from business into politics, and, quite often, back to some key role in bureaucracy. It is wonderfully flexible. The Establishment can, as it has been doing in the mid-sixties, sit back and ponder the changing situation in Asia and the South Pacific while considering how best Japan's interests will be served. Or it can accelerate political and economic policies and go for hegemony in Southeast Asia with a speed that will make the world gasp.

Although it is very old, the Establishment has benefited in the last twenty years from a shake-up in Japanese social structure. War and defeat reduced, although they did not eliminate, the importance of families and titles. These are no longer overridingly important as an entree to the Establishment. What counts now is a degree from Tokyo University, an institution that for the Japanese has the prestige that Eton and Harrow, Oxford and Cambridge, all combined, would have for an Englishman. The University is the source of a "meritocracy" receptive to new ideas, infinitely energetic, avid for improvement, and almost frighteningly certain of its future.

At Tokyo airport, on my departure, I spent a pleasant half hour talking to three young University students all intent on improving their English. One would be a teacher, one intended to go into government, by which he meant the civil service, and one would become a chemical engineer. Comparing them with Americans of the same age, what impressed me most was the absolute certainty with which they talked of their futures and their apparent indifference to anything that did not contribute directly to their training for those futures. Each explained carefully how a command of English would help, and they made it plain that they understood that as a people the Japanese are poor linguists and that this national disadvantage must be overcome by their generation. They had found, incidentally, that English English was a more precise tool than American English.

I have no doubt that in a decade or so these young men will be rising members of the meritocracy, fluent in English and moving steadily toward the home in the suburbs, the membership in the golf club, and the tour of the United States that appeared to represent the best that life could offer them.

Understanding of the Establishment is necessary because it controls a formidable structure of finance, business, and commerce that is easily the most impressive in Asia and one with a far greater capacity for growth and with more adaptability than is found in Britain, West Germany, or France. It is a structure in which the zaibatsu, the financial, industrial, and business complexes broken up by the Allied Occupation authorities in the immediate postwar period, are moving rapidly toward reorganization.

There is an ominous air of the thirties about this development. The Mitsubishi group has been reorganized into Mitsubishi Heavy Industries. The Mitsui combine, while I was in Tokyo, was working to bring together Tokyo Shibaura Electric, which produces electrical and electronic equipment, and Ishikawajima-Harima, a shipbuilding and industrial machinery concern. A multi-product electrical and electronic complex is also in the making under the guidance of the Sumitomo group, which already has acquired a controlling share in Meidensha Electric Manufacturing.

The rationale for the increase in the number of corporate mergers is the conviction of Japanese industrialists that they must either widen their scale of operations or be bested in competition with foreign giants, the word "foreign" in this case meaning United States. But since the zaibatsu were one of the motive forces behind Japan's drive into China and Southeast

Asia a generation ago, most of the elder businessmen thought it necessary to reassure me that the zaibatsu would never again regain their old behind-the-scenes influence on government.

The younger men thought this unnecessary. They took it for granted that Americans know that "Japan has learned its lesson."

Behind the mergers and the revival of the zaibatsu lies the realization on the part of industrialists and their planners that much of Japanese industry needs structural reform. Shigeo Nagano, president of Fuji Iron & Steel, Japan's second largest steel company, shook his fellow tycoons when he advocated the integration of all of Japan's steel producers into two large companies. Elsewhere in the industry, mergers have brought together smaller companies making special steels.

The recession of 1964–65 was the first serious check suffered by Japanese industry since its revival after the war. The damage was not lasting. Since 1966 there has been general progress, with synthetic fibers and electronics, two of Japan's growth industries, spurting ahead. Production also expanded in automobiles and shipbuilding.

Japan, then, is a great industrial power. The question of what she does with this power is of vital importance to her neighbors, Communist and non-Communist.

Like West Germany and Britain, Japan must export her industrial products and buy much of her food abroad. But here again the industrious Japanese are improving their position. The rapid increase in agricultural technology has brought about a continued rise in farm yield. The farmers, traditionally conservative, are increasingly eager to use new farm machinery, particularly power tillers and tractors, and to employ more effective chemical fertilizers. Rice production is envisaged at the level of 13 million tons, the highest in Japan's history. The government expects that as a result it will be able to reduce rice imports by about half a million tons.

With both industry and agriculture expanding, Japan's trade boomed. Exports for 1966 were expected to be around 10 billion dollars, a rise of 1.5 billion in a year. Imports for the year were also expected to run about 10 billion dollars.

The steady expansion of exports reflects the efforts made by Japanese industry to strengthen its competitive position by modernizing management and improving technology, by exploiting markets in Europe and North America, and by taking commercial advantage of the escalation of the war in Vietnam and a rapid rise, there, in the demand for Japanese products. Imports, too, rose because of an increased demand for raw materials and fuel from an expanding industry.

Although the United States is Japan's single largest customer, trade with the Communist countries flourishes, representing 6.5 per cent of the total trade in 1966. Trade with Communist China fell slightly in 1966, owing to the disturbances of the Cultural Revolution, but the total was expected to be around 600 million dollars. Trade with the Soviet Union rose during the year to an estimated 500 million dollars.

There were many indications in Tokyo that Japanese exporters had become wary of trading with the turbulent China of the Cultural Revolution. China did increase its purchases of Japanese chemical fertilizers, some steel products machinery and equipment, in 1966 and 1967. But the Japanese were also doing very well out of the Vietnam war. Exports to South Vietnam rose steadily through 1966 and 1967.

Japan's current export drive offers a prime example of the manner in which the Establishment, without any overt signal, can turn to and achieve a national objective. Diplomats, politicians, and government officials all are deeply involved. Conferences at the ministerial level with foreign countries, notably the United States, France, and Canada, are seized as opportunities for widening the sales of Japanese goods. Japanese

27

ambassadors give top priority to the expansion of exports.

The Japanese concede weaknesses in their industrial structure. There are still too many backward companies among the smaller industries. There is not enough rationalization of major firms. Not enough is done to encourage exporters of capital equipment.

Yet, in the words of one American economist in Tokyo, the "Japanese economy is at the third stage of its rocketlike journey; there's no idea of a slowdown. The progress of the next decade will make that of the past seem commonplace."

Two impressions left by the Japanese economy:

1. It is so closely tied to that of the United States that any American economic collapse would have a drastic effect on Japan.

2. As a power base, the Japanese economy dwarfs that of more pretentious countries like France. But it is a power base with, as yet, no clear international political direction.

The most popular and, of course, reassuring comment of most Americans is that the Japanese appear to be "just like us." This is nonsense.

Superficially, the Japanese do resemble the Americans to the extent that all industrial peoples today resemble each other. But the Japanese character has deeper roots than the country's post-war experience, roots that go back two thousand years. If there is a strong resemblance in character to any western country it is to Britain, especially in attitudes toward the outside world. The reader will have noted the emphasis placed by the Establishment on the expansion of Japanese trade. This has had its counterpart halfway around the world in the British Isles, where for twenty years the country has been urged by a succession of governments to expand exports. The Japanese Establishment has been far more successful than the British. Nevertheless the similarity between two island peoples, striving to live by what they export,

28

dependent on imports for raw materials and food, and willing to trade with anyone, is striking.

"The first lesson any foreigner must learn in dealing with the Japanese," a foreign diplomat long resident in Japan said, "is that when they say 'hai' [yes] they do not mean that they agree with you, but only that they understand."

This is good counsel in estimating the extent of the Japanese political commitment to the United States. My own impression was that American officials, in both Washington and Tokyo, are taking too much for granted in their campaign to establish Japan as a leader in Asia that would more or less faithfully follow the United States lead in the world.

One difficulty that is bound to arise can be traced to the absence of a concept of equality among nations in the Japanese outlook. To be successful, leadership in Asia, especially Southeast Asia, will have to rest on this idea of equality, of first among equals. The Japanese still tend to see countries on the "winner-loser" scale. They, themselves, clearly the loser in the Pacific war, accepted inferiority to the United States and worked their way back to a position of economic power in Asia. But they are unlikely to consider or treat as equals countries like Burma or Laos or Malaysia.

In some ways they are a remarkably insensitive people. No one I talked to in Tokyo seemed to have any fear that, should Japan decide on a political role in Asia, the Japanese would encounter resentment arising from the atrocities committed by her forces in World War II. The attitude seemed to be not unlike that in Germany in the late forties: the country had paid for its sins through widespread devastations and humiliations, and the score was now even; why should anyone resent the reappearance of a people so publicly punished?

"Of course we made a mistake in trying to impose the East

Asia Co-Prosperity Sphere," a young Mitsui executive said, "but we all realize that now, and it is unlikely to be any great barrier to expanding our trade with the rest of Asia."

One Japanese diplomat confided that in his opinion the most difficult, and underestimated, barrier to any future development of Japanese leadership in Asia was his people's difficulty with foreign languages, especially English.

"I have read widely among English and American authors," he said slowly, "but I find it difficult to ask for a cup of coffee when I get to Washington."

Another diplomat deplored the manner in which Japanese difficulties with English, the lingua franca of most of Southeast Asia, gave the Indians an edge. The Indians, he said, "talk and talk and talk at international meetings in fine Oxford English. The Americans understand them. The British understand them. And the Indians walk off with the good international jobs. While we, representing a powerful country, are left on the sidelines."

There is a striking difference between the company manners of the Japanese and their ruthless drive in business and finance. These two aspects of the Japanese face are hard to reconcile. So is their ferocity in war with the amiability and courtesy to the stranger.

"I've known them for forty years and yet every day something reminds me that I don't know them at all," an American businessman said. "Sometimes I believe they're the smartest, busiest, most ingenious people I've ever met. And sometimes they seem like a lot of damned fools."

A few days before, he reported, he had picked up one of the afternoon papers and read a story about a Japanese police exercise devoted to catching a bear, should one escape from the Tokyo zoo. A picture showed one policeman swathed in a bearskin surrounded by his colleagues with nets and clubs. Interested, my friend called up the police to ask if there had been many

30

escapes by bears at the zoo. Never, was the proud reply, but there might be one day and it was just as well to be prepared.

Japan is preparing now for a re-entry into the world scene. The preparation is cautious. But in the Foreign Ministry, in the banks and headquarters of industrial companies, among the politicians, it was quite evident that Japan sees an opportunity in Asia. The problem for the United States is that the Japanese may not be seeing exactly the sort of opportunity that is evident in the State Department. My feeling was that when and if Japan begins to exert leadership in Asia it will be no more acceptable to Washington than France's attempts to do the same in Europe.

Caution pervades the present Japanese approach.

The government now favors economic cooperation between Asian states as the first step toward any establishment of an Asian power group that would, Washington hopes, balance the power of Communist China in Asia. To Tokyo, Asia is divided into two groups of states. One, including Thailand, the Philippines, South Korea, and South Vietnam, wants political as well as economic cooperation. The second includes those states that reject all political cooperation, Burma and Cambodia, and others like Singapore that are tepid about the subject.

No one in the Foreign Ministry, from the Minister, Takeo Miki, down, wanted Japan to take the initiative in forming either an economic or a political group. They were willing to concede that the initiative should be Asian, not American. But at the moment they thought they were not the right country to take it. Why? Well, Japan's economic and political ties with America are so strong that any Japanese initiative might be thought to be the result of orders from Washington. This, it was said blandly, was not the "correct posture" for Japan.

Yet it was evident that these men were under polite pressure from Washington to take an initiative, and that they were

31

desperately searching for some policy that would satisfy the Americans and at the same time preserve their freedom of action.

Perhaps, Mr. Miki suggested, economic help in the "broadest sense" should be the first step. This would cover technological assistance, education, and medical aid up to 1 per cent of Japan's national income. Combined with loans to Southeast Asian states enabling them to buy Japanese goods, might this process not raise the standard of living in the area to the point where its societies were no longer vulnerable to Communist penetration?

A few days later a Japanese official who had sat in on my meeting with the Foreign Minister led me aside at a cocktail party.

"I hope you understand what my minister was saying to you," he said. "It was simply, 'Please, don't hurry us.' He says it all the time, especially to Americans."

The Japanese want time for two reasons. They are very anxious about the Cultural Revolution in China and are more involved in it, psychologically, than any other Asian state aside from Nationalist China. The spectacle of the Chinese giant, now armed with nuclear weapons, threshing about in an apparently uncontrollable delirium worries all Asia. But nowhere, not even in Burma and India with their long frontiers with China, is the anxiety greater than in Japan. And it is unjust to say, as Japan's critics do, that this anxiety springs from a fear that the Cultural Revolution will continue to reduce Japanese export trade with China. Trade is important to the Japanese, but not as important as all that.

Japan's anxiety over the Cultural Revolution tells us a good deal about the Japanese. They have a very strong sense of order and stability. They are bewildered by the spectacle of their huge neighbor convulsed over what the practical Japanese considers minor ideological issues just when China should be directing all of its efforts toward economic expansion. The Japanese are affronted by photographs from China showing respected authors and intellectuals pilloried in dunce caps by the Red Guards. The Red Guards themselves appear to Tokyo as demented children whose wild mouthings of the works of Mao Tse-tung have taken the place of the classic teachings of an older China.

For it was that older China that gave Japan so much of her religion, culture, and language. Since the dawn of history the two peoples have lived side by side in Asia, sometimes at war, more often at peace, linked in an indefinable Asian kinship. While rejecting communism themselves, the Japanese saw, or thought they saw, in the People's Republic a government that would end seventy-five years of turbulence on the mainland. They were willing to trade with the Communists. They believed that in time the passions evoked by the long civil war with Chiang Kai-shek and the enmity toward the United States would subside and China would become a responsible power.

No doubt the economic argument played a part. Here was a country moving toward a population of one billion and needing just about everything Japanese industry could produce. As a trading people, the Japanese saw their developed economy as the perfect complement to China's developing economy. Now, unexpectedly, the political and economic vision lies in ruins. The majority of the Japanese leaders in 1967 had little doubt that the Great Proletarian Cultural Revolution would go on for years. The emphasis would change, they thought, but the Revolution's consequences, a turbulent, irresponsible China whose foreign policy is continually affected by internal disturbances, would have to be dealt with for a decade and more to come.

Naturally the Japanese see a potential political advantage to themselves arising from the Cultural Revolution. To most officials and diplomats, the revolution has taken China out of Asian affairs very much as the treason trials and purges in Russia reduced her influence in Europe in the late thirties. Japan remains as the strongest, most coherent nation in East Asia, with wide opportunities for leadership—if she wants to take them.

But this political advantage is more than balanced by the constant worry over what China will do next. Even a stable China, armed with nuclear weapons and the rudiments of a missile delivery system, would worry the neighboring Japanese. Now, however, they must face a situation in which their giant neighbor is not only armed with these weapons but follows a dangerously unpredictable foreign policy. In these circumstances Japan is more dependent than ever upon American military protection and perhaps more amenable than in the past to identifying Japanese policy with that of the United States in Southeast Asia.

The Japanese government's attitude toward the Vietnam war began to change in 1966 when two conditions became apparent to Tokyo. The first was that the United States was not going to be driven out of South Vietnam. The second was that the expansion of the American military effort that made the first certain was not likely to lead to the entry of the Chinese into the war. As a close ally of the United States the Japanese feared China's entry, thinking it would ultimately involve Japan because of the American naval and air bases in the islands. These fears still remain. But they have been greatly reduced by events.

It was quite evident, however, that the ordinary Japanese have not gone as far as their government in open support of the war. Where the government has no illusions about the character of the war, seeing it as the result of North Vietnamese aggression, many Japanese consider that the war is entirely the result of the intrusion of American power in Southeast Asia.

They see in Vietnamese resistance to the American superpower something from their own recent past: a small country standing up spiritedly to a large one. For firmly implanted in the mass mind is the picture of a heroic Japanese struggle against over-whelming American might in World War II. Although this picture conveniently omits the Japanese aggressions that began the war, it is perhaps understandable in a people whose national belief in themselves as a warrior nation has been so drastically humbled.

Opposition to the war in Vietnam seemed more a matter of the heart than the mind, and it was by no means universal. The Cultural Revolution across the sea awakened Japanese to the dangers of the world they lived in. Consequently when the Americans stepped up their bombing attacks and the U.S. Navy shelled coastal targets, there were no organized demonstrations outside the United States Embassy. These have been standard operating procedure for the Japanese left-wing parties in the past. But the Left, sharply divided by the Sino-Soviet schism, has lost some of its influence. Here we see the effect of the Cultural Revolution, which has linked communism to disorder and in-stability in the minds of many Japanese, on the Left's prestige and influence.

Like all governments in the area, the Japanese would like to see the war ended. However, Foreign Minister Miki's attitude toward a settlement was intentionally ambiguous.

Any open negotiations on peace, he suggested, should be pre-ceded by a private "secret" agreement on the future of Vietnam and on the dividing line between North and South Vietnam. South Vietnam's government, he considered, should deal with the Viet Cong individually, not as part of a general settlement with Hanoi.

The eventual settlement should be guaranteed by the major powers, he said, and Japan would wish to participate in any negotiation. But Japan could not give a guarantee of Vietnam's independence because the treaty with the United States forbids sending Japanese troops out of the country.

These cautious views were those of a minister whose government was poised between familiar dependence on the security treaty with the United States that provides Japan with a nuclear umbrella and movement into the uncharted area of national self-defense and a leadership role in Asia.

The existence of the treaty has been an enormous advantage to Japan. True, it provides for the stationing of American forces in Japan, a situation which the Left complains ensures Chinese enmity. But the treaty also has enabled the Japanese to proceed with their industrial recovery without the necessity of spending huge sums for defense. This, of course, is the sort of passive benefit that usually escapes popular attention.

The security treaty aroused violent opposition when it was adopted. Some Japanese politicians and foreign diplomats believe this opposition will revive in 1970. After that date either party can denounce the treaty after giving one year's notice. Unless a considerable measure of political stability has returned to Asia by 1970, the Japanese seem unlikely to denounce the treaty.

They are, however, thinking in terms of stronger defense, conventional and nuclear. This started in 1966, when the Government Defense Agency began to formulate the third five-year defense plan. Until then Japan had established an 180,000-man army with a reserve of 30,000, a navy of 140,000 tons of ships and 235 aircraft, and an airforce of just over 1,000 planes. The new plan would add 15,000 men, 70,000 tons of new ships, and some hundreds of new aircraft to the existing force. The total armed forces still would be dwarfed by China's millions.

But there is now open, lively discussion in Japan of recourse at some future date to nuclear weapons. Their possession would reduce the enormous disparity between Chinese and Japanese strength.

"Mr. Damon Runyon, who is a great favorite of mine," said

a Japanese general, "used to talk about a pistol as the 'old equalizer' that eliminated the physical difference between the big man and the little man.

"Well, today, there is an equalizer in weaponry, the bomb. With our industrial capacity and our scientific and technological advantages, we could build defensive nuclear weapons that would reduce the danger of Chinese nuclear blackmail. But, of course, these are political decisions with which I have nothing to do."

Some of the discussion about the possibilities of nuclear armament may be attributed to the apparent Japanese reluctance to appear as a stooge of the United States in the eyes of Asia. But more, I think, can be ascribed to the reviving sense of national identity. The Japanese in 1967 and 1968 are going through a psychological change not unlike that which overtook France in the first heady days of General de Gaulle's rule after 1958, when the General's trumpetings about national glory awoke responsive echoes in so many French hearts. The difference of course is that French power weighs very little on the international scale except in nuisance value. Japanese military power, backed by advanced science, technology, and industry, would weigh heavily on the global as well as the Asian scale.

Already the Japanese realize that, as the leading industrial, financial, and commercial power of Asia, their country can be the focus for any movement toward economic and political cooperation in the arc of countries that swings southwestward from Japan to Burma. But, as Foreign Minister Miki's comments made clear, they are moving warily in this area, with trade and aid emphasized before politics. Foreign ministry officials who urge that Japan increase Southeast Asia's share of her total foreign aid outlays to 70 per cent sounded very convincing in Tokyo.

Japanese officials and businessmen seem to be underestimating the impetus behind the trend for regional cooperation in Southeast Asia. Later in that area I was told repeatedly that the Japanese were not doing enough, were not showing sufficient receptiveness to the ideas for regional cooperation that were circulating among the foreign ministries of the countries involved.

Yet any examination of the development of regionalism in Asia shows that the Japanese have played a strong if cautious role. Characteristically, the Japanese were not the originators of the movement. Its genesis was the revival in March of 1966 of ASA (Association of Southeast Asia), composed of the Philippine Republic, Thailand, and Malaysia. ASA, founded in 1961, had been on the shelf as a result of strained relations between the Philippines and Malaysia because of the former's claim to Sabah in Borneo.

Credit for the revival was given to Thanat Khoman, Thailand's Foreign Minister, who judged the moment right for something more than gestures toward solidarity among free Asian states. Mr. Khoman's first action at the ASA conference in Bangkok was to appeal for an Asian initiative to end the war in Vietnam.

Japan entered the picture in April when the Southeast Asian Ministerial Conference on Economic Development was held in Tokyo. The conference was attended by Malaysia, the Philippines, Singapore, Thailand, and South Vietnam as well as Japan. Indonesia and Cambodia were represented but did not openly participate.

The proceedings demonstrated the contradictions of the Japanese position. Japan promised to extend credits of 60 million dollars to Thailand and 50 million dollars to Malaysia and to devote 1 per cent of her gross national product to foreign aid. But the Japanese were cool to a suggestion from Prince Souvanna Phouma, the Laotian Premier, that Japan act as the catalyst in starting a movement toward Asian federation. There were murmurs in Tokyo business circles that a Japanese initiative might harm trade with China.

A second and more extensive Asian federation also came into being in 1966. This was ASPAC (Asian and Pacific Council), formed at Seoul, South Korea, in June and composed of Japan, Malaysia, the Philippines, South Vietnam, South Korea, Taiwan, Thailand, Australia, and New Zealand.

The original purpose of ASPAC, as envisaged by the South Koreans, was an anti-Communist defense alliance. The idea never got off the ground. The Japanese and the Malaysians indicated they opposed militantly anti-Communist groupings, while Australia and New Zealand affirmed their faith in the South-East Asia Treaty Organization, which includes among its members the United States and Britain.

But, since all the members of ASPAC oppose communism with varying degrees of fervor, the final communiqué did call for "greater cooperation and solidarity among the free Asian and Pacific countries in their efforts to safeguard their national independence against Communist aggression or infiltration, and to develop their national economies."

Since then Japan has been a little warmer in her attitude toward Asian regionalism, possibly because, despite a great deal of talk, very little tangible has emerged.

Two courses are open in the future. Japan can move wholeheartedly into the development of regionalism in East and Southeast Asia, gradually assuming the role of leadership of the non-Communist powers which Prime Minister Jawaharlal Nehru sought for India, with the support of American liberals who knew nothing about Asia, India, or Nehru. Or Japan can pursue her own national interests. This will entail providing aid and then credits in the form of "soft loans" of long duration and low interest rate. This program undoubtedly will promote Japanese

39

trade in the area and, ultimately, Japanese political influence.

It is too early now to say which course Japan will follow. What can be said is that before long the restless dynamism of the Japanese is likely to be expressed in a foreign policy far more significant to the future of Southeast Asia than the "low posture" followed by Premier Eisaku Sato throughout 1966 and 1967.

The question asked so often and so earnestly in Washington—will Japan form the center of a new power group balancing China?—remains unanswered.

What is no longer in doubt is Japan's intention to play a more active role in the international politics of the Far East than it has in the last decade. The tour of Southeast Asia in the autumn of 1967 by Premier Eisaku Sato was in the nature of a reconnaissance of the governments of the area: how did they feel about Japanese aid and trade, how real was the movement toward regional groupings, what were the prospects for holding the line against the North Vietnamese in Laos, Thailand, and South Vietnam?

Meanwhile Mr. Miki continued to talk about what he called the "Asia-Pacific sphere," a relationship in which the more advanced countries of the area would assist in the development of the others. Since the advanced countries of the area are the United States and Japan, this was not precisely what Washington had sought in urging greater involvement in Southeast Asia upon the Japanese. Still, the beginnings of a more active Japanese policy could be discerned behind Mr. Miki's words.

"It is high time that not only Asia but also the whole of the Asia-Pacific nations awakened to a sense of solidarity and set about cooperating in the grand task of developing Asia," he said. "From this point of view, I am resolved to devote still greater effort to Japan's diplomacy toward the Asia-Pacific region."

At the same time the Foreign Minister told Japanese financiers that they should begin cooperating with American, Canadian,

Australian, and New Zealand interests in investment programs in Southeast Asia.

Japan, the third industrial power of the world after the United States and the Soviet Union, clearly is prepared to move. A country literally bursting with energy lies next to a great, largely undeveloped, continental land mass. The opportunities for commercial expansion are obvious. Less obvious and probably more difficult to achieve are the possibilities of political leadership. In both respects Asia needs Japan. Will the Japanese be able to sublimate their own feelings of superiority, their own growing nationalism, in the great effort to establish a balance to China in Asia?

III

The God of War Hates Those Who Hesitate

Nothing could be as far from war as the lounge of the Peninsula Hotel in Hong Kong. The tables were filled with garrulous tourists from Brisbane and Los Angeles exchanging information about the wonderful bargains to be found in "cute little shops" on side streets. A group of Englishmen downed their before-lunch cocktails, speculating idly on the afternoon's horse races. This was not the East but the West, transplanted in all its complacency and easy-going materialism. A little Chinese bellhop, neat and smiling in his white uniform and white pillbox cap, came up to say that the taxi was waiting.

In a few hours I was outside Saigon airport. The night was close and hot. For the first time in many years I heard in the distance the rolling rumble of artillery fire. Above, bombers and transports flew on missions of war. The behavior of soldiers and civilians alike showed that odd mixture of tenseness underlying a jesting bravado that animates people at war.

"Jesus, Charlie," a soldier said, "we'd better get back to base or that pistol-assed lieutenant will chew us out good."

Back to the wars.

It is a good idea for any visitor to get out of Saigon as often as possible. Saigon is very like any wartime capital. There are overtones of London in 1940 and 1941, of Cairo during the desert war, of Paris after the liberation. The same furious search for pleasure on the part of young men recently returned from the daily confrontation with death. The same fiercely military attitude of the headquarters and supply personnel. The same bored, slightly cynical "we know better than the soldiers" approach of the civilian officials. The same sort of rumors and gossip, the same silent struggles within the military and government structures for place and power. The faces you see in the bars and in the restaurants are different, but the talk is very much the same as it was in any of those cities in that other war that now is so far away.

The officers and men at the helicopter base display that casual competence that distinguishes this American army. The take-off is set for 6 A.M., and at one minute after the hour the helicopter rises. As it swings north, Saigon, all off-white, rose, and green, lies below, caught by the first rays of light from the east.

As the sun rises the land unrolls below. Villages, towns, cities. No sign of war. On the right the sea and then, suddenly, the great base at Cam Ranh Bay: mile upon square mile of equipment, stores, and weapons laid out in the sun with the sparkling sea beyond. Marveling at this profusion, thinking back to other days in another war fought, at the outset at least, on scanty resources, the visitor suddenly realizes that there is no attempt at concealment, at dispersal there on the ground. Huge gas trucks stand bumper to bumper along the highway. From the air two or three antiaircraft emplacements are visible. Later in the day the chopper slides downward over the base of the 4th Division. Again, the same profusion, the same lack of concealment.

It occurs to the visitor that if the enemy wanted to hit the bases with five squadrons of MIGs some morning, he could change the face of the war in as many minutes. You remark on this to a general later in the day. Cheerfully, he says you're right but "They won't; it's not that sort of a war."

The sort of war it is becomes clearer in the steaming afternoon when another helicopter drops the visitor at a battalion headquarters hacked out of the jungle in the hills near the Cambodian frontier. To the American soldier of the Vietnam war, fire bases such as this are as familiar as the trenches were to the doughboy of World War I.

The trees and the brush have been leveled over a couple of acres. At one end of the roughly rectangular clearing are six 105-millimeter guns. Scattered across it are dugouts, their roofs stoutly sandbagged. Piled nearby are captured North Vietnamese weapons. Dust rises from every footfall. The heat, the damp oppressive heat of Southeast Asia, lies over the base like a sodden blanket. The sweat runs in rivulets down the brown, naked back of the soldier guiding the visitor to the battalion commander, a massive, genial Hawaiian.

The battalion, he explains, has been pushing a North Vietnamese regiment for five days: groping for it in the jungle, locating a picket here, a company there, hitting the Vietnamese with automatic weapons fire, artillery, bombers, and heavy machine guns in helicopters.

"We kill fifteen, twenty, twenty-five a day for sure," the Hawaiian said. "Those are the bodies we count ourselves. But each of these jokers carries a rope with a loop at one end. When they have the chance, they loop this around the foot of the nearest corpse and haul him away. Don't want us to find him, you see. Often we find a body still holding a rope attached to another body. Funny war, eh?"

As we talked an enemy mortar began to lob shells into the jungle beyond the western edge of the clearing.

"Watch Charlie, now," said a Negro lieutenant, evidently much amused. "He thinks he's on to something. He'll mortar the hell out of that one spot. Won't shift. You know, when you're out after them on patrol, they're right smart. But most times, on things like this—that's a big Russian mortar—they're not. They keep firing and our artillery and the choppers will spot him. You see . . ."

From behind us came the outrageous clamor of the 105's.

44

There was a spatter of automatic fire somewhere in the jungle. At the headquarters dugout the commander was listening to a report from a chopper.

"Same bunch," he said. "They got the mortar. They're moving toward the Cambodian frontier. Once they're over that, it's good-by. Maybe we can catch some of them before they get to the river."

"That river ain't going to hold them up none, Major," a captain said. "Hell, I could jump across it."

In this part of the war, the constants are the heat, the dust, and the jungle. The jungle tells you what the word "impenetrable" means. You cannot see and, oddly, although it seems silent, you cannot hear with accuracy. For the jungle is full of small sounds, creakings and scrapings and murmurs, the call of birds, the rustling of some small animal.

A sergeant says, "In here, you gotta be God-damned fast getting in the first rounds. And you gotta be careful it is Charlie." He swung around as a body crashed through the brush to the rear.

"It's okay, Sarge," said a voice from the jungle. "The choppers say they're pulling back."

The sergeant was twenty-three. Here he was leading a patrol, reading maps, calling for artillery fire and bombers. It is that kind of war; this is a professional army. And it is this professionalism, from the high command down to the rifle companies, that is the most striking difference between this army and the one that started for Germany through the African back door a quarter of a century ago. That army, from staff to G.I., had to learn and train as it fought. It was the army of Kasserine Pass, of Gafsa, of Kairouan and of Hill 609 and Bizerte and Tunis. It learned from its mistakes. But mistakes were made, and sometimes they were costly.

This army, never fully appreciated at home and, because of

45

differences over the war in the United States, never receiving the full, vocal support given that earlier army, performs with a cool competence in a war that demands more individual leadership from platoon and company commanders, more independence of thought on the part of the private soldier, than any the army has known since the Indian wars.

For this is a war of groping in a jungle as wide as the sea for an enemy who fights only when he wants to fight—that is, when he thinks that conditions favor him. The kind of fighting the war demands seems particularly suited to the American character, requiring, as it does, a high degree of mechanical competence with light weapons and a rapid, energetic response to fast-breaking situations.

To cope with such situations the soldier's reaction must combine the ability to think for himself with an ingrained discipline. This is, in a rather odd way, a much better disciplined army than that of 1942. The discipline, however, is not of the old spit-and-polish kind that the Regulars of twenty-five years ago tried—and failed—to inculcate, but that of the careful artisan, the disciplined, comprehending mind behind the weapon.

It is a better educated army. Educational standards have risen in the United States in the last quarter of a century. This may in part explain the literate sergeants, the reasoning riflemen. But it may be, too, that the opposition to the war in the United States has led this army to think and talk more about its purpose and its operations than that other army did. This army is attentive to orders and, I think, quicker to understand them than the other.

According to the popular American idea, this army is drawn from a generation notably soft and pampered. Yet one of its most striking characteristics is good physical condition maintained under climatic conditions that are usually appalling.

The officer corps, too, has a broader background and is better trained than the one that led Omar Bradley's II Corps in Tunisia and Sicily. Then it was not uncommon to hear a general complain that he trained his staff as he fought his battles. In this army most of the staff officers have done service in the field. Consequently the old hostility, half joking but half serious, between staff and field officers is disappearing.

It is a serious, even studious army. In Hong Kong I met a group on leave in a bookshop. A bookshop! A Negro sergeant said he and his companions were looking for textbooks to help them prepare for college when they were "out."

The attitude toward opponents of the war at home ranged from profane contempt to indifference. Most soldiers felt that unless those at home came and saw the war they were in no position to judge. They were not talking about big issues, holding communism in check or the future of Southeast Asia, but of the things they had seen.

"You find some nice old Joe, who's talked to you, with his throat cut by Charlie or a couple of village girls ripped up the middle, it makes you wonder whether you're fighting men or animals," a 1st Division soldier said. "You ever see one of these villages after Charlie has worked it over, Jesus!"

The army, although it does not accept the views of the opponents of the war, is attentive to those that have them.

"Of course, you have to pay attention to people like Kennedy and Fulbright," a marine lieutenant said. "They're elected. But they don't know anything about this war."

The individual conclusion in most cases was that unless the critic at home had lived through the experiences of the average man at the front, his criticisms would, in the mind of the soldier, be largely invalid.

The G.I.s of a generation ago were often highly critical of "Franklin D. Roosevelt's war," and so were many of the National Guard officers. There is little similar criticism of President

Johnson. Not that the army has forsworn bitching. There are plenty of gripes about the food, the mail service, the dust, "the lousy pilots who never put the stuff where we want it."

Morale has stood up remarkably well, I believe because of one salient difference between today's army and that other army. The soldier of 1942 was "in," as far as he knew, until he was killed, wounded, or the war ended. The soldier in Vietnam is there for a year. He thinks he knows the approximate date when he will be "out." Like Americans of every generation he does not, with some notable exceptions, like the army. But being in it, being there for a scheduled period, he makes the best of it. His understanding that he is there because of the Vietnamese enemy makes it very tough for the enemy. For this American is a very competent and skillful soldier.

Late one night I talked to a 1st Division colonel, a friend from the old days in Germany.

"These kids can take anything and they can lick anybody," he said. "Whatever people at home think about the war, they should be proud of this army. There's no 'death or glory' stuff to it, you know. They just do what they have to do and they do it damned well."

The man who commanded this army when I was in his way was a striking departure from the generals of World War II. General William C. Westmoreland spent a great deal of time at the front, and by that I do not mean some lavishly furnished corps headquarters within sound of the guns but in fire bases in the jungle, in the rice paddies of the Mekong River delta, in the dusty scrub of the plains, and in silent, timorous villages. Quite often he intervened in actions fought at the battalion level or even lower. And that night he would be back at his headquarters reconciling what he had seen in some unnoted fire fight with the big picture as it was charted on the huge maps.

Now a general who operates in this manner is certain to attract the gibes of other commanders. Repeatedly the visitor was told, "Westy's trying to do too much" or "Westy's letting the staff run the war, while he plays soldier." Such criticism does not seem to affect men like Westmoreland; they are much less sensitive than the generals of a generation ago and, I think, much more confident of their abilities. This was true not only of General Westmoreland but of the staff and the corps and divisional commanders. Perhaps there is too much confidence. Some of the predictions of enemy defeat seemed, to a visitor, surprisingly unrealistic. But in fulfilling the primary function of the military service, that of simultaneously planning and carrying out an operation and instantly reacting to the thousand and one things that inevitably go wrong, no matter how detailed the planning, how good the troops, when the action moves from the maps to the firing line, these commanders seemed to me as competent and as skillful as the men they commanded. And this is high praise.

The easy assurance of the commanders in the Far East comes naturally. They, unlike the Eisenhowers and Bradleys, never knew the poverty-stricken, undermanned army of the years between the World Wars. The greater part of their military career has been spent under conditions of military opulence in a large, active, well-equipped army. Their background includes courses at Harvard Business School and staff colleges and training with a big, well-found Seventh Army in Germany rather than tarpaper bungalows and down-at-heel barracks in forgotten posts with companies simulating battalions on maneuvers.

World War II, Korea, the army in Germany, NATO have made this generation of American commanders familiar with international politics and diplomacy. Every generation, of course, makes its own mistakes. But it would be surprising if this one were to handle the political situation in Saigon as badly as Eisenhower and General Mark Wayne Clark did the one, equally delicate, that arose in Algiers after the Allied landings there in 1942. During this period General Clark genially informed reporters that he and Eisenhower referred to the French, with whom they were negotiating and who were soon to become allies, as "YEBSOBS." This he explained stood for "yellow-bellied sons of bitches."

Such mulishness is unheard of today. The army has learned its way around the diplomatic world; its leaders are at home in the presence of statesmen and diplomats.

But in their attitudes toward the popular approach to the war, the commanders display a rather attractive but possibly dangerous ingenuousness not apparent when they are dealing with the larger issues of international affairs. To men trained to believe in the West Point concepts of "Honor, Duty, Country," agitation against the war, especially agitation by students and their professors, is almost incomprehensible. To them the burning of draft cards and the carrying of North Vietnamese flags in parades borders on treason. They were almost totally unaware of the profundity of the sentiments of the opposition and they despaired of the Republic. It was not easy for them, or for anyone else who has been at the front, to grasp that the same generation could produce both the "hippies" and the calmly efficient young soldiers at the front.

General Westmoreland's attitude toward the nature of the war was that of the seasoned professional soldier. He saw it as two inextricably connected campaigns: one against the Main Force—that is, the North Vietnamese Army—and the other against the Viet Cong guerrillas. To the American military leaders, the first is the more attractive. It is the war of major operations, the fighting in which professional military reputations will be made. To the average West Pointer, and there are far more Academy graduates in Vietnam than in the armies of World War II, anti-guerrilla operations are of passing interest. Lee is still a bigger name than Nathan Bedford Forrest.

To many state department and other officials, however, *the* war was that against the Viet Cong. They criticized the command in Saigon for concentrating on "the big war" against the Main Force. They argued that, although it is conceivable that allied operations in the field and the continued bombing of the north will force Hanoi to reduce Main Force operations drastically, this will not win the war against the Viet Cong.

The professional's answer was that once the Main Force attack is punished so severely that Hanoi reduces the scale of operations, the allies will then be able to turn a much greater share of their strength against the Viet Cong.

Until that is possible, however, there will almost certainly be a sharp difference in allied progress in the two wars. The second war, the guerrilla war against the Viet Cong, is not the "big" war in terms of men involved but it certainly is in terms of area. The battlefield is everywhere that the South Vietnamese government does not rule; the combatants and noncombatants include close to 50 per cent of the total population.

In the guerrilla war, fought mainly in the countryside, the Viet Cong or, as they call themselves, the National Liberation Front rely on food seized or extorted from peasants; they assemble weapons in hide-outs, train recruits, all behind the friendly curtain of the jungle. Taxes are levied in areas held by the V.C. and also in those sectors where the peasants fear the guerrillas will return unless tribute is paid.

The V.C.'s tactics are as old as war, the tactics of every guerrilla force against a better-armed enemy: sniping, ambush, assassination of village elders and government officials. The sporadic nature of the attacks and their geographical extent give the impression of a spontaneous uprising against the government in Saigon and its American friends. Nothing could be more ad-

51

vantageous, politically, to the North Vietnamese and the woolly-minded sympathizers who consider the war a civil war. Nothing could be more wrong.

The guerrilla war in South Vietnam is run by Hanoi and has been since 1956 when President Ho Chi Minh began to send guerrillas south to reinforce the Communist-trained Viet Minh already in South Vietnam. Le Duan, Ho's chief political adviser, deals with the general strategy of the guerrilla war. Lieutenant General Nguyen Van Vinh controls the supplies sent south to the Viet Cong. There are at least five North Vietnamese generals in South Vietnam directing operations against the United States.

The entry of the United States into the war in force in 1965 almost immediately changed the guerrilla fighting. The V.C. now faced a more mobile enemy whose firepower far exceeded anything encountered heretofore. Since then, although the number of "incidents," terroristic attacks on individuals, has risen to about twenty-five thousand annually, the guerrillas have been much less successful in encounters with regular American and allied troops. During most of 1967, V.C. casualties rose, recruiting declined, and the infiltration of reinforcements from North Vietnam were reduced by the bombing of the Ho Chi Minh trail and by the manpower requirements of a battered North Vietnamese economy.

What keeps the V.C. going? The same political calculation, I believe, that sustains Hanoi. This is that the United States will not bring in the reinforcements the Communists consider necessary to successfully fight both the Main Force and the Viet Cong. This, in North Vietnam's estimation, would require an expeditionary force of over a million men. Escalation to that extent in a presidential election year is out of the question. Consequently Hanoi will be able to continue the war on both the regular and guerrilla fronts convinced that during or after the election campaign the American people will tire of the war and its sacrifices and force withdrawal upon whichever party rules in Washington.

This is the logic of the situation as seen by the Communists and by many of their sympathizers in Western Europe. Plausible although it may be, it omits, like most Communist logic, unpleasant realities such as the fact that the North Vietnamese, the driving force of the war, now are suffering heavier casualties than the allies. It also discounts the possibility that the American reaction to a continuation of the war may not be what Hanoi wishes it to be. Instead of withdrawal the American people may demand a more intensive and extensive prosecution of the war that would leave Hanoi and Haiphong in rubble.

The conflicting opinions over military priorities on the American side are one of the conditions that complicate the war. Equally important is the geographical condition that, while it exists, will prevent the allies from accomplishing their aim of forcing the North Vietnamese to reduce the scale of their operations.

This geographical condition is the continued neutrality of Cambodia and the use by the North Vietnamese of eastern Laos for supply routes. Repeatedly, North Vietnamese forces, under heavy American pressure, have withdrawn across the frontier into Cambodia to rest, re-equip, and replace casualties. The North Vietnamese ability to retire into this Cambodian sanctuary is as important an advantage to Hanoi as the hospitality offered its fighter squadrons over the northern frontier in Communist China. When these factors are considered with the movement of North Vietnamese reinforcements, replacements, and matériel through Laos and through Cambodia, the geographical condition emerges as one of the most important advantages enjoyed by Hanoi.

The situation is deplored by senior American and Allied officers throughout the theater of operations. There is nothing they can do about it. But as long as the enemy enjoys these advantages, the American military effort will be gravely handicapped. If the war is to be pursued as vigorously as the services would wish, some time President Johnson and his advisers must face the harsh fact that winning the war, in the sense that North Vietnam is moved by military pressure to negotiate, becomes improbable in the light of this situation.

This is not a situation widely discussed in the United States outside of the Pentagon. It is discussed in almost every capital in Southeast Asia where America's willingness to allow Prince Sihanouk, Cambodia's Chief of State, to play the Communist game to the detriment of United States' interests is a matter of regret. To people facing the immediate threat of Communist aggression, there are no equivocations.

Nothing I saw or heard confirmed the impression, widely held outside Vietnam, that we are dealing with a completely dedicated foe. Certainly the North Vietnamese leaders have displayed great courage and ingenuity. But the interrogation of prisoners and captured documents are evidence that the rank and file on the other side is neither as efficient nor as enthusiastic as North Vietnam's supporters would have the American people believe. There are persistent complaints that the Americans are too numerous, too well armed, that the American artillery and air force make it impossible to concentrate for an attack or exploit any local success. There are complaints from officers that replacements are badly trained and have no interest in the war.

After one takes into account the obvious competence of the American forces, their advantages in matériel and their superiority in the air and at sea, the nagging question remains: why aren't they doing better?

The primary reason is that the United States and its allies are defending a state, South Vietnam, that is not an integrated state. They hold only a fraction of the country, and that fraction's

54

people have little sense of national identity. Goaded by the United States, a succession of military juntas has tried to inculcate national feeling and to build a stable political base through national elections and the establishment at all levels of government of a facsimile of democracy. The military leaders have introduced a program of agrarian reform that includes the sale of government-owned land to peasants. They have trumpeted the slogan "social justice." But they have quite clearly failed to inspire the army or the people it represents to make the sacrifices of energy and endurance that the situation demands. They have neither the affection nor the respect of the people.

Premier Nguyen Cao Ky may well have vanished into obscurity by the time this appears in print. In April of 1967 in Saigon he undoubtedly was the most important and controversial Vietnamese in the capital. Most of these discussions about the war and its future in which Americans whiled away the long hot nights included, at some point, the remark, "Now, if we had someone better than Ky."

I've heard that sort of remark a hundred times in a dozen capitals during and since World War II. To me, it reflects a curious political naïveté. For, surely, although it may be preferable to have someone better than Ky—or Darlan or Badoglio— as head of the government, the question really is whether there is anyone better who will serve effectively. The man does not always match the hour; Cromwells and Washingtons are hard to find. The natural American desire to see our Vietnamese allies led by a heroic, international figure must conflict with the harsh historical truth that in such situations nations must work with what they have at hand. Given the continuing struggle between the armed forces and the civilians for power in the South Vietnamese government, and the Vietnamese character, Air Marshal Ky appeared about the best we could expect to get.

Of course, his appearance is against him. He is too young,

too smooth. The day we talked aboard U.S.S. *Enterprise* his immaculate pilot's flying suit was touched up by a lavender scarf at his throat. In the company of a group of American generals and admirals he was almost too much the bright pupil, the industrious apprentice saying all the things they wanted to hear.

Yet there was an obvious sincerity when he talked of his country and its problems. Yes, he conceded, he and his fellow generals could be considered a military clique "by outsiders." But who else was there? "The junta has the support of the people, whatever people like Mr. Walter Lippmann think, and only the military can build a democratic South Vietnam.

"Why do we have popular support?" the Premier asked. "Because we know and say that what the country needs more than anything else is social justice and the people understand this. For a century they have wanted land reform. We are providing it. The government that will be elected this autumn will carry out wide reforms. You will see. We are better men than those people in America think."

Understandably, Premier Ky is obsessed by communism. This arises from his own experience in fighting communism and his conviction, common enough among the leaders of Southeast Asia, that communism and aggression are identical. And if he has any thoughts about compromising with communism, and I am convinced he has not, these would soon be eliminated by his dealings with the American officers with whom he comes in contact. The armed services of the United States have been planning to fight Communists for twenty years. To their senior officers communism remains *the* enemy. They cannot understand and in many cases do not believe that anyone in Washington could even consider compromise.

Mr. Ky, then, is an articulate, persuasive fellow. The gap, however, between program and performance is too wide. The land reform program has impressed many South Vietnamese farmers. But there was a notable lack of enthusiasm for the Premier and his fellow general officers in the junta. Instead there was a deep suspicion of all government. For in South Vietnam as in so much of Asia, government is synonymous with corruption, repression, and nepotism. Time and responsibility may cure this. But it is not to be ended by cheery handouts from the United States Information Service or speeches by Premier Ky. Here again, Americans must work not with the ideal but with the rather sordid reality.

It was a relief, after listening to the Premier's emotional oratory, to talk to Dr. Tran Van Do, the Foreign Minister. Elderly, unassuming, highly sophisticated, Dr. Do saw his country's and Southeast Asia's problems against a wider background.

For example, he thought that no final settlement involving the withdrawal of the North Vietnamese and its "puppets" of the National Liberation Front would mean anything unless it was supervised by the United Nations or some other international organization "with the cooperation of our own people."

"Obviously, outsiders cannot say who is and who is not a Communist," Dr. Do commented.

Moreover, the Foreign Minister insisted, there must be an international guarantee of South Vietnam's independence once the war ends.

"But we don't want French involvement in that guarantee," he added. "The French are useless. They told us we could trust SEATO [South-East Asia Treaty Organization], but when we needed SEATO, the French pulled out."

Even an international guarantee would be risky, Dr. Do pointed out. It would be easy enough for the guarantors to act in the event of open aggression against South Vietnam by another state or states. But how, he asked, would the guarantors agree to act against subversion? Would a Communist power —he had Russia in mind—agree to counter-subversive actions even if it were a guarantor of South Vietnam's freedom?

"The only way in which we can prevent subversion in the long run," he said, "is to improve our economic and political situation. We are doing that. But it cannot be done quickly. And you Americans want everything done immediately. We are too old a people for that.

"So it is with regional groupings in Southeast Asia. They will come. With the Chinese and the North Vietnamese as they are, they will have to come. But that will take time, too. In the end we will stand on our own feet.

"I often ask myself, what will be the best thing we can do once this long war is over and peace and security have been restored. Clearly, we must ask the Americans to go—troops, bases, everything. For then we will be truly independent and then we will prove to the world that we can build a stable state.

"After all, the United States doesn't need bases here. With modern technology, bases are obsolete. And the presence of bases and troops created problems for us. We have been an occupied country too long."

Dr. Do sighed. "But you know, when the war does end here, it will not end everywhere. You must be prepared to support others as you have supported us. Not with soldiers, I hope. Not in battle. But with economic and technical aid. We will all need that if we are to resist the next Communist campaign against Southeast Asia."

I have quoted Dr. Do at length because his words symbolize what is moderate and wise in the Saigon government. He represents the type of man that must figure prominently in the future of South Vietnam and, indeed, of all Southeast Asia if that future is to be hopeful.

The goals the United States has set in South Vietnam are simple. They are to halt the aggression by North Vietnam, through its Main Force and through the National Liberation

Front and Viet Cong that it directs and supports, against South Vietnam and to restore security and stability to the country.

But if these goals are comparatively simple, the conditions that impede American attainment are infinitely complex. The first and by all odds the most important of these is the political weakness of the Republic of South Vietnam. The government is not the collection of power-mad militarists, intent only on power and personal enrichment, that opponents of the war portray. It numbers in its ranks many farsighted and energetic ministers and officials trying to do something for the people. But it is not the sort of government that inspires popular support and confidence. Until these develop, there will be no firm political base.

The absence now of such a base clearly affects South Vietnam's military contribution. Some elements of the armed forces are good, particularly the marines and the airborne units. But in general the forces are poorly officered and lack a sufficient number of experienced noncommissioned officers. This condition will not be cured by sending more and more American military advisers to the Vietnamese forces and sending more and more bright young Vietnamese to American staff colleges. It will not be cured by new weapons. It will change only when the ordinary Vietnamese in the ranks believe that their Republic is worth fighting and dying for.

The conclusion must be that until the South Vietnamese themselves are fit to play a role equal to that now played by the allies in defending their country, the allies, and particularly the United States, will carry the largest share of the military operations. The army, air force, and navy of the United States are today and will be as long as they are there the main barrier to the Communist subjugation of South Vietnam.

The second condition that bars the attainment of America's goals is the use by the enemy of neutral Laos and Cambodia. As long as the territory of these states offers both sanctuary and

59

supply routes, the military situation will not develop to the position where the North Vietnamese forces are so badly punished that they are forced to reduce their operations. I left South Vietnam convinced that, were access to Laos and Cambodia denied the enemy, within a year the North Vietnamese would be so hurt on the field of battle that their campaign would begin to decline in intensity and scope. But as long as the Cambodian frontier is open to the North Vietnamese and closed to the allies, as long as reinforcements and supplies can move to the battle areas through Laos and Cambodia, the American effort, on its present scale, will suffice only to check the enemy's aggression.

The third condition is the restrictions placed on the American air offensive on North Vietnam. These were imposed for political reasons that seemed justifiable to the President and the National Security Council and the Chiefs of Staff at the time. When this is read, they may have been modified. But in the spring of 1967 it was quite evident that these restrictions reduced the effectiveness of American air operations.

Seeing a war at first hand, and then, later, seeing it as millions of Americans at home see it through television and the newspapers, emphasizes the peculiar psychological problem facing a nation fighting a conflict that is not formally a war. In many of its aspects the American military effort has been far more successful than the average American seems to realize.

One aspect, which goes almost unrecognized in the United States, is the rise in morale, the stiffening of purpose among America's friends and allies in Southeast Asia as a consequence of effective U.S. intervention in Vietnam. It is impossible and intellectually dishonest to think of the war solely within the boundaries of North and South Vietnam. To do so is to miss the importance of the conflict to other peoples.

Two attitudes have developed in the United States that are potentially dangerous in a situation as grave as the present one.

First there is the tendency to seize upon, emphasize, and often exaggerate every American reverse while minimizing as "propaganda" every American or allied success. The second, and perhaps more important, is the "can't win" philosophy, the idea that the Republic is doomed to a decade or more of unrewarding expenditure of men, money, and matériel. Let us try to put this war into its true perspective, which is the present and future in Southeast Asia.

There are no popular wars, certainly among those who fight them. There are, however, wars that are inevitable under the circumstances. The war in South Vietnam is one. If the Americans withdraw from South Vietnam without first establishing its independence and territorial integrity, the rest of independent Asia is unlikely to fall apart immediately. But I am convinced that should the United States, weary of the war, scuttle out of South Vietnam then, within a relatively short period, five years at the most, Communist pressure would be renewed, perhaps against Thailand, perhaps against Burma, perhaps in northern India.

The United States could not ignore the challenge. But the effectiveness of its response would be reduced. What would be the position then of the South Koreans, the Thais, the Laotians, the Filipinos, the Malaysians, and the others who now support us? How would they respond? It is entirely probable that in the interval, having judged in view of our withdrawal from Vietnam that American promises mean little, they would either have come to terms with the aggressor or withdrawn, as Burma has already done, into a defenseless neutrality. Parenthetically, those who clamor for withdrawal might occasionally give a thought to what would happen to those Vietnamese now at our side. Withdrawal would surely condemn hundreds of thousands of them to death or Communist prison camps.

This war can be considered one that, if successful, will buy

AMERICA'S STAKE IN ASIA

for our allies in Southeast Asia and for others who need it time to build their political and economic defenses against future Communist pressure. We are fighting as much for the future of these peoples as we are for our own, perhaps more. The Vietnam war is hard enough to fight with allies at our side. Another war, fought on our own, would be infinitely more difficult. We cannot expect help in Asia from the British, the French, or our other NATO allies. We must make do with what we have, the peoples of the area who cherish their independence. If we withdraw from Vietnam without establishing its independence and security, we will surely lose their help in any future crisis.

The war in Vietnam is unpopular. The war is hard. The war is fought under terrible handicaps imposed by geography, by political restrictions, by the weakness of the Republic of South Vietnam. But it is a war fought with some advantages, ports and access to the American bases in Japan and the Philippines. These advantages would not be present in a war fought, say, in Burma or India. To say that it is not the right war, at the right time, in the right place is to beg the question. There never was such a war.

Yet when the plane lifted me out of Saigon en route for Vientiane, I could see no other course than that the United States has chosen. Accepting the handicaps, exploiting the advantages, conscious of what the re-establishment of an independent South Vietnam will mean to the rest of Southeast Asia, we must stay and fight.

Victory, in the sense that most Americans think of the word, is out of the question. We cannot and should not think in terms of unconditional surrender by North Vietnam. We can and should think in terms of the defeat of North Vietnamese aggression in the south and the restoration of independence and security to South Vietnam.

To say that the United States cannot do this is a counsel of despair. To say that it should not is to ignore callously what assuredly will happen to independence and freedom in Southeast Asia if we withdraw. "There are no easy options in war," Lord Alanbrooke used to say. There are no easy options for America in Southeast Asia. We can stay, at a high cost, and ultimately achieve our goals through great national effort. Or we can go, and assure that although this generation of Americans may win a few brief years of complacent peace, the next, and perhaps the next following, will be doomed to an unending conflict in Asia. If this War of National Liberation can be won by the allies, we can expect Peking to reconsider its support for such wars in the Indo-Chinese peninsula and elsewhere in Asia. But if the war is lost by American withdrawal, we can almost certainly expect further Wars of National Liberation around the perimeter of China, wars that will involve us either because of treaty obligations or because of clear national interest.

That is the war. Those are the stakes. The answer does not lie with the G.I.s out in the fire bases or with President Johnson, Ultimately it lies with the American people. This has been their century thus far. But if they opt for appeasement in Vietnam, the remainder may belong to someone else.

IV

Laos, Malaysia, Thailand, Singapore: The Heart of the Problem

Four states, Laos, Malaysia, Thailand, and Singapore, are the heart of the problem of Southeast Asia's future. If these four can retain independence and freedom, improve their economies and social structures, and move gradually toward some form of regional grouping, there is hope for the future. Such progress requires a period of relative stability in which the North Vietnamese are held in check and the Communist Chinese are too preoccupied with their internal differences to devote their full energies to Wars of National Liberation.

Two of these states, Laos and Thailand, already are grappling with Communist enemies. In the spring of 1967 and throughout most of that year the two governments were more than holding their own. Each of these guerrilla wars, however, demonstrates what the Communists would like to accomplish there and elsewhere in Southeast Asia.

"All revolutionary peoples will learn to wage a people's war against U.S. imperialism and its lackeys," Marshal Lin Piao proclaimed on September 3, 1965. "They will take up arms, learn to fight battles, and become skilled in waging a people's war, though they have not done so before."

What the Chinese call a "people's war" has been going on in Laos for a decade. Far from being a popular war spontaneously supported by angry peasants, as pictured in Peking's mythology, it is in fact a war fought by a Communist army, the Pathet Lao, supported by North Vietnamese regulars against the recognized and legitimate government of the country. The war in fact is an extension of Communist imperialism with the North Vietnamese

64

already claiming parts of Laos as theirs. Because it is being fought in Laos, which borders on Thailand, and affects the insurrection in that country, this little war is of continuing importance to the stability of the entire area. Success for the Communists in Laos would seriously worsen the allied position in South Vietnam, face the Thais with a hostile Communist state on their northern frontier, and encourage Communists in Malaysia and Singapore. The war that flickers through the jungles and over the mountains of this strange and majestic country, then, is one whose outcome can affect the fortunes of three stable, relatively prosperous states.

All morning we had flown across the heavily forested tumult of land between Saigon and Vientiane, the administrative capital of Laos. Now we came out above the Mekong River plain and below us lay Vientiane, dusty and baking in the noon sun. Across the Mekong was Thailand.

Laos is a country about the size of Norway, with a population of between two and a half and three million. Its people have been at war, with only a few short breaks, since 1939. The war has not been a total war, of course. Only small numbers of men have been engaged on both sides. But its cumulative effect has been terrible in so small a country: young men killed, crops ruined, villages burned. The Laotians are a mild and merry people, but they have the underlying strength of so many Asians that enables them to pick up the pieces after each disaster and doggedly rebuild their lives.

Prince Souvanna Phouma, who is as near to being the indispensable man as one can find in Asia, thought when I saw him that the war was going fairly well. In 1964 his government had controlled only half of the national territory and between 30 and 40 per cent of the population. Now he said, the government holds two thirds of the country and 80 per cent of the population. Of course, he added with engaging frankness, these figures can be deceptive because no one controls large areas of the country. However, he added cheerfully, the government controls the Mekong River.

The Prince is the only man with the character and prestige to keep the competing factions in his government working together. He knows his country and its people and, more important for Laos, he knows the outside world and its strains and stresses.

To that world Laos is, in theory at least, a neutral country, so established by the Geneva Agreements of 1962. Again in theory, it is ruled by a coalition of Communists, neutralists or centrists, and rightists. In fact, the Communists, the Pathet Lao, and the political front have withdrawn from the government. The Pathet Lao forces are fighting the government of which, in theory, their political representatives are a part. It is, the Prince remarked dryly, a strange world.

But to the Prince and his followers, the Pathet Lao is not the true enemy. The North Vietnamese, he said, force the Pathet Lao to continue the war, although the latter has little military capacity and has lost whatever political appeal it had in the past.

At this point a young and obviously nervous civil servant entered. Excusing himself, he said there was something wrong with one of the statistical diagrams sent over from the ministry. Would the Prince look at it? The Prince sighed, put down his pipe, made the necessary corrections, and resumed the conversation. This is part of the pattern of Asian rule. A conversation with President Ferdinand Marcos of the Philippines was interrupted by three farmers from a remote village angry over the lack of progress in a government project in the village. The President took ten minutes to reassure them.

Laos is under attack in two areas. To Americans the more important is that in the east, where Laos borders on North and

South Vietnam. It is there that the Ho Chi Minh trail skirts the Demilitarized Zone's western end. Along it march the troops who reinforce the North Vietnamese and the Viet Cong in the battle areas. It is symptomatic of North Vietnam's aggressive and expansionist policy that the Hanoi government now claims that the area of Laos through which the trail runs is Vietnamese territory.

The second southern supply route, through the port of Sihanoukville in Cambodia and up the Mekong to transhipping points near the Vietnamese-Cambodian frontier, is outside Laotian territory. But the Royal Laotian Air Force, trained and supplied by the United States, does what it can to reduce traffic down the Ho Chi Minh trail. Both Laotian air force officers and the United States Military Mission in Vientiane concede that, while these attacks make what the latter called "an appreciable dent" in the traffic, it is impossible, with the present resources, to interdict the flow of men and matériel southward.

Meanwhile the Royal Laotian Army has been inching its way toward the eastern frontier. Gradually more farm land has been recovered. Villages have been rebuilt.

The army's successes, there and in the north, have been won mainly over the Pathet Lao. The pattern is an attack by North Vietnamese, usually aimed at rice stocks, followed by the garrisoning of the area by the Pathet Lao. The royal army then attacks and drives back the Pathet Lao. Prince Souvanna Phouma thought that the army now was attacking "more vigorously" and that the Pathet Lao troops were far inferior to those that fought against the government in 1960 and 1961.

He estimated that there were about thirty thousand Vietnamese troops in Laos, many of them untrained conscripts. Did he want international intervention to drive them out? No, he said, wearily, that would mean an expansion of the war and Laos "has had too much war; just give us time and matériel and we will win." By 1968, he predicted, the government would have recovered even more territory in the farming areas.

In the northeast, a wild area of mountains and jungle far different from the placid plain of the Mekong, at least eight hundred thousand Laotians still live under the rule of the North Vietnamese. There the government operations are aimed at regaining at least one half of the Plaine des Jars, a fertile area, and turning it into farmland. A success here might be the political and military breakthrough the Prince has been seeking for the last three years. It would also benefit the United States.

Trucks shuttle back and forth through the northeast, especially in Sam Neua province, bearing heavy equipment for the North Vietnamese and the Viet Cong. Many of the stocks of heavy mortars and recoilless rifles that reached the front in 1967 traveled over this route. By truck, by barge, by coolie, supplies flow steadily southward. Again, the re-establishment of the royal government's authority in the Plaine des Jars would not interdict this traffic, but it clearly would reduce it.

Like Vietnam, this is a war of battalions and companies, fought for isolated villages with names like Nam Bak. An attempt to capture Nam Bak was, for Laos, a major operation in early 1967. About ten battalions were involved on both sides, but in the end the North Vietnamese were able to hold their positions. Throughout 1967 the war continued: ambushes, skirmishes, raids. The Laotians lost 177 men killed in action and 542 wounded or missing in the first three months. It is not a big war but it is an important one.

"The lash of the dragon's tail" is a phrase that crops up in discussions of the war in Laos. It refers to the possibility, never far from the minds of Laotian leaders and American diplomats, that the North Vietnamese, their plans for South Vietnam frustrated by the United States, will turn westward and engulf all

Laos. Should that happen, the Communists will stand astride the northern frontier of Thailand favorably placed to feed the insurrection they have started there from the security of new bases in Laos.

Laos, of course, is not where the United States wants to fight —if it has to. President Kennedy, in 1961, saw that if communism was to be checked in Southeast Asia, American naval and air power could be used to greater advantage in Vietnam than in landlocked Laos. But a combination of North Vietnamese greed and strategic supply considerations has kept the war going. Men creep through the jungles, field guns roar in jungle clearings, and the little T-28 propeller-driven bombers skim over the tree tops along Ho Chi Minh trail searching for a truck, a marching column, a barge.

In Vientiane the Prince-Premier works late into the night. Sometimes when he wants a break he will stand by the open windows looking out at the sleeping town. To him it is "all one war, what we do here, what the Americans do in Vietnam, what the Thais do across the river. We must make the North Vietnamese realize that they cannot win, that this part of Asia intends to remain free."

To the south across the Mekong, isolated villages hear the Communist chant:

> "Awake, awake, people,
> To see blood for blood.
> We are victorious soldiers.
> Victory is won by the farmers,
> Capitalism and feudalism will fall."

Here, again, the North Vietnamese are at work. The leaders of the rebellion in Thailand have been trained in Hanoi. They are supported with food and information by the North Vietnamese settlers in northeast Thailand. The guerrillas move in bands of twenty to fifty men through seven provinces, Ubon, Udon, Nong Khai, Nakhon Phanom, Sakon Nakhon, Kalasin, and Loei. The Phuban Mountains are their stronghold and from them the guerrillas sally forth to assemble as many as one hundred men, armed with automatic weapons and grenades, for attacks on government troops or, more usually, helpless loyal villagers.

Major General Sayud Kerdphol, Chief of Operations for Thailand's Communist Suppression Operations Command, estimates that there are about twelve hundred guerrillas constantly in the field, with another six thousand in the villages with concealed arms. He thought that the movement, the United Patriotic Front of Thailand, can count on another five to six thousand unarmed sympathizers.

The traffic in arms is part of the way of life in Southeast Asia from Burma to the Philippines. The guerrillas get arms directly from the North Vietnamese and the Chinese and buy other weapons from deserters from the Laotian army. But the Communists, despite the accessibility of weapons and initial surprise, have not been successful.

They do not have well constructed bases in deep jungle but must operate mainly in what, for Southeast Asia, is largely open country. Nor, General Kerdphol said, is there evidence of coordination between various localized independent groups.

Talking at his headquarters in the inaptly named Rose Palace, the General outlined the Thai plan to contain "the C.T.s," Communist terrorists.

The first step was to select the ten areas most sensitive to guerrilla activity and send in Thai army platoons supported by two counterinsurgency companies. The guerrillas, who depend on sympathizers for food, have to operate fairly close to the villages. They soon found that they, the hunters, were being hunted by the Thai troops. The guerrillas were forced to move away into areas where villagers were unfriendly and they could not count on food and information.

In these circumstances the number of guerrilla attacks fell early in 1967 and the number of propaganda meetings also declined. So did assassinations of loyal village leaders. Assassination is a tactic in this war as it is in Laos and South Vietnam; kill or intimidate the local leaders and the Communists will gain ground.

With the arrival of Thai troops, loyal villagers have become bolder. Backed by platoons of regulars, they refuse to help the Communists. Most villagers at the outset are neutral, the General admitted, but once the security forces move in they have a shield against coercion by the Communists. If the guerrilla attack develops into something too big for the troops on the spot, then what the General called "the reaction forces," heavily armed companies, move into the fight.

"The reaction forces and vigorous patrolling have kept the C.T.s moving since January of this year [1967]," he explained. "They have begun to harass the C.T.s. As long as they are kept moving it is hard for them to get food; as long as they are on the run they are cut off from their relatives who might give them information. We garrison about two hundred and fifty villages in the key area.

"We hold the area and we maintain our grip on it," General Kerdphol added. "We do not go away."

How big a war? Small enough by the standards of this century. But, like the other wars in Southeast Asia, it is of deadly importance to the area's future. In 1966, thirty-seven officials, village leaders, and teachers were assassinated, as well as seventy villagers. There were 127 clashes between Thai forces and the Communists, eighteen ambushes of government troops, and one attack on a government building in Udon.

Thailand's long-range plan is to establish security in the villages and at the same time to raise living standards.

"We want to encourage other government agencies to interest themselves in the civic and economic side," the General said. "But it will take a long time.

"The C.T.s think that time favors them and that we will go away. But we will stay five, ten years. Not just one year."

The two great impediments to an early end of the war are the proximity of the Mekong River and the North Vietnamese settlers, a community of between forty and fifty thousand in northeastern Thailand. Originally refugees, these North Vietnamese have never abandoned their loyalty to Hanoi.

Although they admit they cannot stop individual guerrillas from crossing the Mekong from Laos into Thailand, the Thai commanders on the spot believe that through better cooperation between the river police and the army they could stop crossings by groups of Communists.

The Communist leaders are mostly Thais of Chinese ethnic origin or North Vietnamese hiding behind Thai names. These latter extract food, money, and information from the North Vietnamese community.

But, according to the General, "moving the North Vietnamese out of the area would solve nothing. What we must do is make them good citizens—and if they are not good citizens, arrest them."

These poverty-stricken provinces in the north are a long way from the opulent capital of Bangkok. Part of the army's task is to convince comfortable bureaucrats in Bangkok that an improvement in the conditions of village life is essential to victory. Loyalty will not be won permanently by military demonstrations or by honors to village leaders. There must be, the officers agreed, a farsighted economic program to raise living standards by bringing farm implements, fertilizers, and insecticides into the area.

To the American commander in Bangkok, Major General Joseph E. Stillwell, no relation to World War II's fiery "Vinegar Joe," this was the most difficult part of the campaign. Here, as elsewhere in Asia, he and his staff saw the situation as a race between Communist attempts to cow and subvert the population and the government's efforts to improve conditions to the point where the peasant, the chief target of the Communists, will actively resist Communist pressure.

The general impression both in the field and in Bangkok in 1967 was that the government's *military* efforts had been largely successful. From the American standpoint, the guerrilla war had convinced the Thai government, which didn't need much convincing, of the danger posed by North Vietnamese aggression. This had led not only to the rather impressive military effort against the Communists but to a good deal of quiet support for Laos, the buffer state between Thailand and North Vietnam. Thai rice has gone to feed the four hundred thousand refugees in Laos from areas held by the North Vietnamese, and Thai arms have been sent to the Laotian army. Small though it may be by United States standards, such aid symbolizes the gradual coming together of Southeast Asian peoples in the face of Communist aggression.

"There are none so blind as those who will not see," and it is a gross oversimplification to compare the insurrection in northeast Thailand with the start of the war in Vietnam. Yet many Americans are all too ready to do so. Curiously, they omit from their comparisons the essential that in each case the war was started and sustained by Communist North Vietnam. But they overlook the great differences between Thailand and Vietnam.

There has never been any territorial division of Thailand. The war is being fought in areas traditionally Thai. There is no division in Thai's Buddhist church over the war. The church supports the government. Thailand, unlike Vietnam, was never

73

a colony, and the Thais, even the farmers in the fields, are out-spokenly proud of their national history of independence. There is little absentee landlordism in Thailand to create discontent among the peasants. Finally, in the monarchy, the Thais have a symbol of unity.

Some Americans are quick to scoff at such symbols. But Napoleon knew that "men are led by toys." Almost every Thai home has one or more pictures of the King and his Queen. Thais will forget their anger at the politicians' corruption—no greater than in most Asian countries—in bursts of vehement loyalty to the royal family.

Thailand and Laos, then, are two countries where the leaders and the great majority of the masses know war against communism not as an abstraction but as an ever-present danger that must be fought and defeated if they are to remain their own masters. This is what they are fighting for. Not for the ideals of democracy but for the simple right to till their lands and keep their shops and sell their wares in the way they wish. Fortunately, as we shall see, the governments in Bangkok and Vientiane have realized that the fight cannot be won solely by soldiers, and slowly—too slowly in many areas—the effort has begun to raise living standards, to see that the farmer gets more from his fields, the shopkeeper has more to sell.

"You haven't heard anyone shout 'stop the bombing' around here, have you?" asked a British diplomat in Vientiane. "And you won't, old chap; these people are right under the gun."

Dr. Johnson's remark, that if a man is going to be hanged tomorrow it concentrates his mind wonderfully, might well be applied to the leaders and the governing and business classes of Southeast Asia.

"The United States feels very strongly that Southeast Asia should be defended against Communist forces that want to

74

dominate the rest of Asia and the world," said Tunku Abdul Rahman, Malaysia's wise old Prime Minister. "So it is in the United States' interest to defend Southeast Asia."

The war in Vietnam won't end, he said with some bitterness, "while half the world sympathizes with North Vietnam. They think the world is backing them.

"But they are the aggressors and they have broken all the agreements. How can the war be brought to an end except by fighting them? Because they don't want peace. If the Americans leave South Vietnam it will be taken over by the Communists, and if the Communists win that battle they will use Vietnam as a stepping stone. The U.S. has no choice, if it values democracy, other than to try to defend South Vietnam."

This elder statesman of the British Commonwealth thought various ideas for a peace settlement in Vietnam impractical. If the Communists wish peace they could do what they have done in Korea and make peace, he pointed out. But they are driven by their ambitions and their belief that the Americans will abandon the war.

The Tunku's conviction that the future of Southeast Asia depends to a very great degree on the outcome in Vietnam was shared by Thanat Khoman, Thailand's Foreign Minister.

"There will be no second Vietnam, no third Vietnam, if the Americans and their allies are successful there," he said. "If we succeed in solving this main problem, the rest will solve themselves. Meanwhile the war in Vietnam feeds other wars; the Vietnamese had to help the insurrection against Thailand because we Thais were helping the Americans. And, of course, they *are* aggressors. What is happening in Laos and northeast Thailand is a natural corollary of what is happening in South Vietnam."

Men of the experience and caliber of Mr. Khoman, the Tunku and Prince Souvanna Phouma, while grateful for American intervention in Vietnam, are a bit puzzled over what they consider the naïveté of the American attitude in the late fifties and early sixties toward Communist expansionism in Southeast Asia. They think, in fact, that America waited too long to intervene, that intervention could have taken place earlier with more immediate effect and at less cost.

And they are mystified, and occasionally angered, by the attitude toward the war of American and European liberals. The focus of their mystification and anger is the often expressed liberal belief that the United States has no place in Southeast Asia and that it would be better to let the whole area fall to communism than to become involved in a long and costly war. The shoe was on the other foot, the Asians say, when aggression menaced Western Europe and the Atlantic community. But aggression's consequences leap frontiers, they argue; successful aggression in Vietnam today could promote aggression in India tomorrow.

"What would the American and English liberals do then about their darling, India?" asked one foreign minister who did not wish to be quoted in this context. "Is aggression acceptable in South Vietnam and Thailand but bad in India? Of course not. Aggression is always evil, and it is as evil in one part of Asia as in another."

He and others could not understand why opponents of the war in the United States and men like U Thant, Secretary-General of the United Nations, could believe that a cessation of the bombing could lead to peace. To their embattled governments, one of the lessons of dealing with communism is that any concession to the Communists is answered not by a Communist concession but by demands for more.

Nor do they accept the theory that the present aggression of the Vietnamese and the pronounced xenophobia of the Chinese are passing phases in national development. In this respect, they believe, the American opponents of the war are too much influenced by events in the Soviet Union since the death of Stalin, believing that because Russia's attitude toward the west developed a greater flexibility in the interval, China's attitude will change as well after the death of Mao Tse-tung.

"It is foolhardy to believe that this will occur in Asia," a Thai civil servant said. "We know these people; they have no sense of the possible. If they believe they are destined to lead the world revolution, and that's what Marshal Lin Piao is talking about, then they will continue to foment that revolution whether Chairman Mao is alive or not. We know them, I tell you. They drove us out of Yunnan, oh, many, many centuries ago."

To the leaders of Southeast Asia, including some who are not quite as outspoken in their support of the Americans, the war in Vietnam and its settlement are inextricably connected with the fighting in Laos and Thailand. Any peace arrangements for Vietnam, they contend, must be expanded to include the two other countries. Any guarantee of independence and territorial integrity for Vietnam must be extended to cover Laos and Thailand and, perhaps, Cambodia as well.

Confining the settlement to Vietnam alone, they emphasize, would be to shut one door and leave the others open.

Comments on American attitudes toward the war on the whole were temperate. This cannot be said of those dealing with General de Gaulle. From Tokyo around to New Delhi, but especially in Southeast Asia, the General's recognition of Communist China—now largely forgotten in the West—and his Delphic statements on the advisability of an American withdrawal from Vietnam were execrated.

"The General just isn't in contact with reality," said Mr. Khoman. "He just doesn't know a damned thing about Asia."

"Folie de grandeur," murmured the sophisticated Dr. Do in Saigon, "but without the grandeur."

"He means no harm," said a Malaysian diplomat. "All he wishes to do is to commit us to Chinese hegemony. That's all."

Prime Minister Lee Kuan Yew of Singapore was less enthusiastic, publicly, about American intervention in Vietnam, not, I thought, because he doubted its necessity but because he has grave misgivings of the United States' willingness to fight the protracted war he considers inevitable. Yet like every other leader in the area that I encountered, he had few doubts about the danger to his people arising from a Vietnamese victory, or Chinese expansionism.

"First let me say that I think that this [South Vietnam] was not the best place in Southeast Asia to have taken a stand," Prime Minister Lee said. "If you had consciously made a choice with the hindsight you now have, I doubt whether you'd have drawn the line as you have in South Vietnam. You've gone in and raised the stakes with every commitment, increasing the price that you will have to pay for failure to live up to your declared objectives.

"The worry is whether your open society will allow you to conduct the kind of battle the South Vietnamese war is going to become—a protracted and bitter battle with no prospects of spectacular or decisive victory."

The greatest danger in the situation, as Prime Minister Lee saw it, was that "of popular pressure growing up around your institutions, your Presidency and your Congress, for swift and decisive victory.

"If you can just hold the situation and prevent the other side from winning," he argued, "you will have made a valuable contribution to the long-term stability of the region. If you cannot resist pressures for a more intense effort and quicker results, then I see grave troubles for the whole of Asia, for the whole world."

Prime Minister Lee, the grandson of a Chinese immigrant,

rules the tiny island state of Singapore. His country is profiting from the Vietnamese war to the extent of about 7 million dollars a month. Yet because the great port looks south toward the Indonesian archipelago and the war is being fought hundreds of miles to the north, he takes a more objective attitude than his opposite numbers in Kuala Lumpur, Bangkok, and Vientiane. His thoughts roved to the future of the United States in Southeast Asia beyond the immediate exigent situation.

"A few years ago," he said, "you [the United States] had a wider range of options. Over the last two years you have gone deeper and deeper into your commitments. The problem really is the wisdom of it all. You have already made the decision. I hope historians looking back will not judge it unwise.

"I don't think that in the seventies the problem of Asia is whether America wants to dominate Southeast Asia," the Prime Minister continued. "Your problem is whether you can prevent it from being added to somebody else's strength. Naturally you want to prevent Southeast Asia from being swung over to the other side. The smaller countries in Southeast Asia would prefer the comfort of their own separate selves, which is only possible if there are countervailing forces like the United States to keep them from falling into the orbit of the larger powers in the continent."

This led Prime Minister Lee to outline Singapore's position on regional groupings in Southeast Asia. This is the most talked about, and potentially the most important, development in the area. The impetus it has gained in the last two years comes chiefly from a general recognition that Southeast Asia must do something for itself if it is to build a society stable enough, politically and economically, to resist political subversion or military interference from the north in the future.

Singapore, Mr. Lee said, "has nothing to lose in joining in regional associations or groups, provided they are not based on ethnic or ideological exclusiveness. And in fact, in the long run, this is the only way in which the smaller and not very viable countries in Southeast Asia can maintain their separate existence in a world dominated by the superpowers."

Southeast Asia as it now is, he conceded, is "fragmented, a target for economic and political subversion," and it must "realize the facts of life" and "get together" with economic cooperation coming first.

The difficulty, he said, is that each nation sees regionalism in terms of its own national interests. The Japanese think of it in terms of the Pacific basin and those countries living on its edge, Japan, the United States, Canada, Australia, and the others. The Malaysians "see regionalism in terms of Thailand, the Philippines, and Malaysia."

"From our standpoint," Mr. Lee said, "the starting point should be a group including Malaysia, Thailand, the Philippines, Indonesia, Cambodia, Burma, and Singapore."

This is a wider and more varied group than the Association of Southeast Asian Nations organized in Bangkok late in the summer of 1967 and comprising the Philippines, Thailand, Malaysia, Singapore, and Indonesia. The inclusion of two neutrals, Burma and Cambodia, precludes any anti-Communist bias for the group.

S. J. Rajaratnam, Singapore's Foreign Minister, while supporting regionalism fervently, warned against expecting too much too soon. Southeast Asia, he pointed out, has to learn "Europe's lesson," that smaller powers must band together if they are to face the superpowers, in the first years of their national existence.

Most countries of the area, he conceded, "are experiencing the joys of nationalism at the moment," but events are forcing them to recognize that to survive independently either as political or economic units is "impossible, illogical; stability and progress can only come from regionalism."

The United States, he insisted, "must" support any steps toward regionalism.

This insistence on American support was echoed by Tunku Abdul Rahman in Kuala Lumpur. He pointed out, however, that although there had been a great deal of talk, there were at that time no projects of any importance that resulted in cooperation among the states of Southeast Asia, although "there is plenty of talk, plenty of schemes."

The aim of the Association of South-East Asia, which the Tunku clearly did not regard as the final answer to regionalism, "was mutual help." But thus far none of the countries involved had done anything but make gestures, he said.

Malaysia's attitude toward regional cooperation is governed to a considerable degree by the line Indonesia takes toward this development. The "confrontation" between the two countries remains a vivid memory in Kuala Lumpur, and, despite the eclipse of President Sukarno, the Tunku and his government remain extremely suspicious of Indonesia's intentions.

If Indonesia entered ASA or any other regional grouping, the Prime Minister said, "it would walk out again if it did not get all the money it wanted."

"My suggestion," continued the Tunku, "which has not yet gained the support of the other countries, is to form an 'Aid Indonesia Club' to get together to see how best we can help Indonesia. The Indonesians are not keen on the idea; they think it would mean a loss of face for them."

There is a marked difference between Southeast Asian leaders' unwillingness to commit themselves fully now to an idea that is still nebulous and the enthusiasm of young men in the foreign ministries for regionalism.

"It's almost a cult at the moment," said an official in Kuala Lumpur," but I hope Americans won't dismiss it as just another wild idea. People are coming to see its value. Obviously, we must create the conditions that will enable us to resist communism. And we must do it ourselves. We want American help but not American interference."

Thanat Khoman sounded the same note.

"The time is long past," he said, "when outside powers can dictate to Southeast Asia. We are moving fairly rapidly toward regional groupings, and we hope the United States will help. But a regional group or regional groupings should not be exclusive. We hope to deal with all powers, but we are not going to accept dictation from the superpowers.

"We in Thailand," he added, "are not as nervous about future American involvement as some of our friends. We have agreed to the establishment of American air bases here because we know that the United States has no idea of occupying Thailand and that it is in our mutual interest to halt aggression in the north."

All proposals for regional cooperation have the same general objective: acceleration of economic growth, social progress, and cultural development in the region through joint endeavor. But having established these obviously laudable aims, the heads of government have done very little thinking about the concrete steps that should be taken to achieve them. There is talk of joint promotion of tourism, a joint shipping line, joint efforts to expand deep-sea fishing—a necessity for hungry Asia—in offshore waters.

Young officials talk optimistically of the prospects of establishing a Southeast Asian common market. The difficulty here is that the potential members of such a market would all rely on sales of raw materials—rubber, rice, woods—to the developed nations. They cannot sell to each other.

The oldest regional organization, the Association of South-East Asia, made up of the Philippines, Thailand, and Malaysia, has made some progress in the sense that there have been intergovernmental talks on pooling air and shipping lines and the reduction of tariff barriers. But here again national selfishness, national ambitions, have slowed the pace.

It is well to recognize the psychological barriers and the economic impediments to the development of regionalism in Southeast Asia. But it is realistic, too, to consider that the pressures generated by North Vietnamese aggression and the constant threat of Chinese political pressure may enable these countries to move more rapidly toward some form of regional cooperation than now seems possible.

Before we view the slow but courageous efforts of the Southeast Asian states to build their strength against an uncertain future, we must examine one community common to all these states, the Hwa Ch'iao, "the sojourners," the overseas Chinese. Ever since the late forties when the European colonial empires in the Far East began to disintegrate and Communist China began to take shape, political developments in Southeast Asia and its economic progress have been affected by this community.

No one could provide exact figures on their numbers. I heard estimates ranging from 10 million to 15 million for the number of overseas Chinese in South Vietnam, Laos, Cambodia, Thailand, Malaysia, and Singapore. Whatever the figure, these industrious, thrifty Chinese have made both a positive and a negative contribution to the countries in which they live. Highly developed skills in finance and trade, including a willingness, rare in the Far East, to advance risk capital, have established them among the area's leading entrepreneurs. Those few who, like Prime Minister Lee Kuan Yew of Singapore, have gone into politics have in most cases been strikingly successful.

The negative contribution starts with the name. They are in name, if not in fact, sojourners, temporary residents, and they are so regarded even when they are citizens in good standing of the states they inhabit. A natural clannishness, a strong racial loyalty, an eagerness for education set them apart from Malays, Thais, and other indigenous peoples. Their business acumen usually is much greater than that of the people among whom they live. At best they are the object of suspicion, at worst of hatred.

Until late 1966 the overseas Chinese suffered from another disability. They appeared to many as the representatives of Communist China, the power that had fomented a war in Malaysia, encouraged the North Vietnamese aggression, and proclaimed its intention of supporting, by propaganda and occasionally by arms and equipment, those Wars of National Liberation it expected to foster across Southeast Asia. They were regarded as spies and enemy agents. The remittances wealthy Chinese sent back to their country were considered evidence of disloyalty to the governments of the states in which they lived.

Feeling against the overseas Chinese in Southeast Asia was exacerbated by the pride with which they viewed the development of contemporary China and by their claims to racial superiority. Many of them had fled a country torn by recurrent civil war and humiliated by European and American domination of its economy. Although not overwhelmingly Communist, these sojourners were at the beginning encouraged and later outspokenly proud of the manner in which China became united by the Communists and, in the fifties, began to make her weight felt in Asia and Africa. The Middle Kingdom, after more than a century of virtual vassalage to the West, now amounted to something; it was a proud thing to be a Chinese.

The outbreak, spread, and intensification of the Cultural Revolution in China, as I have indicated, has been one of the strongest political influences encouraging other Asians to desperate efforts to consolidate their economies and strengthen their political structures. Central to this development is the idea that the Cultural Revolution, by concentrating Chinese attention on the internal struggle, has given the rest of Asia time to prepare for future resistance to Peking pressure. The reader will, I hope, bear with me if I re-emphasize that the developments in China and the American success in halting the destruction of South Vietnam by the North Vietnamese are considered the two most hopeful events in Asia from Tokyo around to Teheran.

One of the most important effects of the Cultural Revolution outside China has been the gradual disillusionment of the overseas Chinese.

Perhaps the best expression of it comes from a young Chinese merchant in Singapore whom we will call Mr. Liu, although that is not his name.

"Neither I nor any of my family are Communists," he began in faultless Oxford English. "But you will understand that we all held our heads a little higher as China seemed to go from strength to strength. They were doing jolly well and answering all those who considered the Chinese finished as a people. I considered, for a short time, sending one of my boys back to China. After all, it was the home of his ancestors.

"But now look at things. Denunciations of leaders. Fighting in the provinces. Men grasping for power. This ludicrous cult of Mao Tse-tung. This hatred of all foreigners. Now letters are unanswered. Those who send remittances have no way of knowing if they are received. This is the China my grandfather fled.

"Last week the senior member of our community called most of us together. He is an old man, dying of cancer. He had expected to return to China and die there. But, he told us, he could not return now to a land that had shamed us—yes, shamed us. He advised us to put aside any ties with China, to think and work for the benefit of Singapore. For it was clear to him that this 'new China' is no different from the old, without honor, dignity, and respect for the past."

The effect of the Cultural Revolution upon the Communist

85

parties of Southeast Asia has been drastic. Those local parties obedient to Peking are receiving little or no direction from party headquarters there while the Cultural Revolution runs its course. Counterintelligence officials in Bangkok, Kuala Lumpur, and Singapore reported an appreciable slackening of activities by "Peking Communists." Foreign Minister Thanat Khoman cited reports that the tumult in mainland China had "created doubt among North Vietnam's leaders over the wisdom of putting too much reliance on Chinese support.

"Even Prince Sihanouk of Cambodia," Mr. Khoman said with a grin, "is beginning to have second thoughts about his Chinese friends."

Communism generally, both the Moscow and Peking brands, has lost prestige and influence in Southeast Asia because of the split between the two parties. The split, as it appears in capitals where representatives of both camps compete, seems irreparable. For followers of Chinese communism, the Soviet government and party are now *the* enemy. If this seems exaggerated, consider that, to the early Bolsheviks, the Menshevik faction in the Russian Communist party appeared far more dangeous than did Czarism and the Imperial Russian government.

One Asian expert on communism said with sober emphasis that "there is a better chance of rapprochement between the United States and Communist China than between China and Russia."

To Prime Minister Lee, ruling an island whose economy is dominated by the Chinese, the Cultural Revolution has "cast down and demoralized" the supporters of Peking.

"What can they do?" he asked. "Whatever they try, China's position will never be the same again. Comrades of forty years are denounced with bitterness, with unbelievable abuse. When the overseas Chinese hear these high, shrill shrieks of anger, what are they to believe about China's stability and progress? You know, in most of Asia the Communists are the oldest political party. Age and their activity during the last days of colonialism won them a certain respect. But not now; that is over. Young people are not turning to communism but to political parties that appear constructive."

The premise on which the governments of Southeast Asia and their European and American helpers and advisers are working is that the area can be made economically viable with the United States providing the greater part of the technological and economic assistance. The critical view of many in the United States is that America should not become involved in a "rundown" area, that the country's principal interests lie in western Europe, that Southeast Asia is the natural area for the extension of Chinese political and economic hegemony.

The great economic issue in the area, however, is not the charge that it is economically derelict. The economies of Thailand, Malaysia, and Singapore and the beginnings of recovery in Laos refute that. The issue is common to the East in general: the struggle to raise enough food to meet the demands of an increasing population. Before we can assess economic futures in the area, consideration must be given to this problem on whose solution all progress depends.

The projected population trends for the four countries under discussion are frightening enough, even though population growth in them is not as great as in some other Asian countries, and Singapore, at least, has made an encouraging start toward population control. Eight years ago its population, now about 1.93 million, was growing at the rate of 4.7 per cent annually. A government program reduced the figure to 2.5 per cent in 1967, and officials aim at stabilizing the percentage at 1.5 in the next decade.

But Malaysia and Singapore, with a population of about 12

million today, will, by the most pessimistic estimates, have nearly 21 million people by 1985. Thailand's present 31 million will have risen to 52.5 million by that date, and little Laos's 2 million will have swollen to 3.275 million. Bad though these figures are, they are dwarfed by expectations in the Philippines, a Catholic state where family planning is almost unknown. There are 33 million Filipinos now. There will be, again at the most pessimistic estimate, over 66 million by 1985 and 100 million at the turn of the century.

Two problems march together: increasing the productivity of agriculture, especially rice farming, throughout the area and restricting population growth.

Of the four countries only Thailand, with a population growth rate of 3.4 per cent each year, is a rice-exporting country. In 1967 it expected to raise 2.5 million tons of rice and export well over 1.8 million tons.

A young American-educated expert in the Ministry of Agriculture in Bangkok, Sala Dasananda, explained excitedly the "revolution" that is changing the Thai peasant from a subsistence farmer into a cash farmer.

"Our program of helping the farmer is finally succeeding," he said. "At first the farmers were skeptical. When we introduced new methods, new fertilizers, new strains of rice, new pesticides, they clung to their traditional methods. But when it was demonstrated that they could grow more rice, that they could sell their surplus, the idea caught on. They work together now, and in the villages you can see the difference. More consumer goods, better clothes. You cannot understand how important this is to us. The government program is costly but worth it."

There is a serpent in every Eden, however, and in Thailand the difficulty is the rising population. Foreign experts in Bangkok expect a rice *deficit* in Thailand in twenty-five years, when the population will be nearly doubled, and, with an increased demand for land, a halving of the present area available to the cash farmer if the birth rate is not reduced by 10 per cent starting in 1970. The government is moving slowly toward a birth control program now. It must move much faster if Thailand's economy is to avoid danger.

But Thailand was the world's leading rice exporter in 1966 for the third consecutive year. The natural tendency in the capital was toward optimism over the present and a Micawberish attitude of "Don't worry, it won't happen" toward the future. In the villages the farmers, happy with new machines, with cash in their pockets at harvest time, were confident. One old man confided, however, that the new methods "left very little time for fêtes and love-making. Believe me, in the old days we had one machine that *never* wore out." At this his wife burst into a shrill cackle of laughter.

Rice, which is the staple food of half the human race, represents the main dietary source of energy throughout southern Asia. More than 200 million Indians rely on rice almost solely for food. Nine tenths of the world's rice crop is grown in the Far East. Yet this crop, valued annually at at least 20 billion dollars, must be increased if the Far East is to avoid disaster twenty years hence.

For rice today is pre-eminently a subsistence food crop, with more than half of the world's harvest of over 250 million tons retained on the farms. As long as this vast tonnage fails to enter commercial channels, the task of raising production to feed Asia is more difficult. Subsistence farmers are less responsive to monetary incentives than commercial farmers. The salient result of the government's program in Thailand has been to demonstrate on a large scale what farmers can do to raise production when they are given the cash incentives and the necessary fertilizers, pesticides, and tools.

The extension of Thailand's experience to other countries,

however, is not the complete answer to the continuing food crisis in Southeast Asia or elsewhere on the continent. A more important step toward that solution has been the development by the International Rice Research Institute at Los Baños in the Philippines of IR-8, a rice strain that may double rice yields throughout the East.

Robert F. Chandler, Jr., the Director of the I.R.R.I., believes that if "all the governments concerned make all-out efforts, doubling the rice yields in ten years is within the realm of possibility." Others are less cautious. The Food and Agriculture Organization of the United Nations reports that IR-8 will give more than 13,200 pounds per hectare (2.47 acres) under trial conditions.

IR-8's advantages include strong seedling vigor, high tillage ability, short stature—"we changed the architecture of the plant," says Dr. Chandler—and moderately early maturity. A disadvantage is the strain's susceptibility to bacterial leaf blight and the rice blast fungus prevalent in the Philippines.

On balance the I.R.R.I. experts consider IR-8 a significant improvement over most of the varieties of rice being grown commercially in tropical Asia. As such it will play a key role in the agricultural revolution that must be won if famine is to be averted. This revolution must do for rice what great technological changes in culture have done for wheat cultivation in the last twenty-five years. But, as they say in Asia, "We haven't got twenty-five years."

For the time being, however, Thailand's capacity to export rice gives the four countries of Southeast Asia under consideration an economic advantage in the form of a fairly reliable food supply. This essential resource has been augmented by the rapid increase in Malaysian rice production at the rate of 45 per cent in ten years. Malaysia's rice imports have fallen from 45 per cent of the total imports in 1948 to 23 per cent in 1966, and here again the introduction of IR-8 under a double cropping system has been the main factor. Government officials in Kuala Lumpur looked forward to Malaysian self-sufficiency in rice by 1975.

Malaysia is a good example of the many countries in Asia and Africa whose economies are at the mercy of world commodity prices. Her two great export products are rubber and tin. In the spring of 1967 tin was no problem, for the world price was high and the market avid. But rubber presented a difficulty.

One ironical reason was that for twenty years, beginning in the days of British rule, the Malayan rubber industry has spent sizable sums on research and development. A Rubber Research Institute has sought to develop high-yield trees and has been strikingly successful. At the same time the Institute has developed processes that suit the needs of manufacturers. Parenthetically it might be noted that while this program was strongly supported by the Malaysian government after independence from Britain, the government of President Sukarno in nearby Indonesia did very little to improve and expand the rubber industry, the chief element in the rich economic heritage left by the Dutch.

The second factor in the rubber problem involves the United States. During the Korean war the United States bought large amounts of Malaysian rubber for stock-piling. But in 1966 the General Services Administration in Washington began to sell some of these stocks on the world market. Although the G.S.A. sales amounted to only 5 per cent of the world's consumption, they affected an already falling world rubber price. In February of 1967 the price of rubber descended to an eighteen-year low.

Despite this, Malaysia continues to be, in the opinion of the United States Ambassador James D. Bell, "the underdeveloped country that is most successful in carrying out economic development."

One reason for the optimism of Mr. Bell and other foreign

91

diplomats is the emphasis placed by Tunku Abdul Rahman's government on the government's plan for economic development covering the years 1966–70. Most governments in Asia have economic plans. Malaysia's works. It has four principal aims.

The first, to promote the integration of Malaysia's peoples and states, is to some extent political. For one of the country's political weaknesses is the imbalance between the wealth of the Overseas Chinese minority and the poverty of most of the Malays who make up the bulk of the population.

Three cultures rub shoulders in a country of 11 million people: the Malays make up about 53 per cent of the population, approximately 30 per cent is Chinese, 9 per cent indigenous non-Malay. Population grows at the rate of 3 per cent a year, one of the highest growth rates in the world.

The Chinese and Indians control a disproportionate share of Malaysia's wealth. Some foreigners estimate it at 90 per cent, although this figure was rejected by Dr. Ismail bin Abdul Rahman, the Minister for Home Affairs. He thought the Chinese and the Indians controlled about half the country's wealth.

Admitting that this imbalance remains the country's "key political problem," the Minister said that "all right-thinking Chinese support our solution of the problem." This is a rural development program that will improve the economy, health, and education of the rural Malays.

To implement the program, enthusiastic young government officials are stirring drowsy kampongs with news of farmlands made available to folk who for centuries have scraped a bare living from fishing and tiny rice plantings hacked from the jungles.

The highest priority has been given to the expansion and diversification of agricultural production and the raising of rural living standards. By 1970, if the present program goes according to schedule, 450,000 acres will have been opened to the farmers in the eleven states of West Malaysia, on the Malay peninsula, and 21, 250 families settled upon them. In Sabah and Sarawak, the two states of East Malaysia, on the island of Borneo, 60,000 and 80,000 acres of new farmland will be opened. Programs in agricultural research, crop subsidies, courses in plant protection, animal husbandry, and forestry development, and the establishment of a bank for indigenous people are all part of the campaign.

Obviously Malaysia faces many problems. Some are political, such as the communal disputes between Malays and the Chinese and Indians arising out of the latter's economic power. Others are economic, such as the reliance on rubber and tin. But Malaysia is a country of compromise. Under a tacit agreement among the races, Malays hold most of the important posts in the government and the civil service, while manufacturing and merchandising for the most part remain in the hands of the Chinese and Indians.

Malaysia is alive, confident, vigorous. There is a throb of life in Kuala Lumpur, Penang, and other cities. A new life is beginning for the peoples of the forest and the shore. Education is expanding rapidly; by 1970 expenditure on education will amount to 5 per cent of the Gross National Product.

The Malaysians display a national self-confidence unusual in Asia. As the visitor is repeatedly reminded, Malaysia has defeated a Communist attempt to overthrow its government. Although generous praise is given Britain for the role it played, then and later in the confrontation with Sukarno's Indonesia, the Malaysians feel that their national contribution was important and perhaps decisive to the victory. "And in twelve years of fighting the Communists," the Tunku reminds visitors, "we learned what our enemies are like."

Singapore's decision to break away from Malaysia and proclaim her independence in 1965 weakened both countries. It came after some years of gradually mounting distrust and suspicion on both sides. Two and a half years after the break, relations between the two countries were strained, superficially at least. Politicians of both countries delighted in tossing shafts of rhetoric across the Strait of Johore that separates the two countries. Yet both capitals conceded the fundamental need for economic cooperation. The bulk of Malaysian trade continued to move unimpeded through Singapore. Presumably it will continue to do so because this is to the economic advantage of both parties. Yet the political antipathy between Singapore, the cosmopolitan city-state, and Malaysia, a chiefly agricultural country, continues.

Singapore's great natural resource is her port. The island's area is 224 square miles or, as officials joke, "225 square miles at low tide." Within this small area a remarkably diversified industry has grown, benefiting from a highly educated, easily trained and adaptable labor force. Throughout the fifties, when Singapore was known as the Red City, this force was too unreliable to attract capital investment. One of Prime Minister Lee Kuan Yew's feats has been to pacify the unions. Another minor miracle of the Lee government has been to establish a government that is unusual in Asia because of its efficiency and because of the absence of corruption and nepotism.

The island boasts a steel mill. Originally built to handle iron ore from Malaysia, the mill now subsists on scrap, largely old ships, and turns out steel bars, pipes, and cables. Union Carbide has built a plant to make batteries and transistors. Other plants turn out building materials, needed by an expanding public housing program, electrical equipment, edible oils, canned goods, veneer and plywood, and even clothes for the U.S. market. The exports to South Vietnam, booming since the start of the war, include fabricated building materials, steel reinforcing rods, and plywood. In the late spring of 1967 this trade was running at about 7 million dollars a month.

But Singapore's reason for being is the port. Through it in 1966 passed goods valued at 2.4 billion dollars. Rubber, coffee, timber arrive from other parts of Southeast Asia to be graded, processed, packed, and sent all over the globe. Singapore is the biggest oil shipping and bunkering port in the world.

This noisy, vivid metropolis has its internal problems. The birth rate, although descending, is still high. A polyglot population—one can see representatives of every Asian race in the streets—presents difficulties. The demands of education and housing strain the budget. Yet Singapore has a brash optimism.

"Of course we have our problems," a young lawyer said. "But one resource can never be taken away." He gestured out at the harbor. "I counted eighty-one ships an hour ago," he continued happily. "Look south, the first islands of Indonesia. Look north, Malaysia and Thailand. As long as we enjoy and exploit this position, we will prosper."

Despite their vigorous independence, both Singapore and Malaysia are friendly to the West. Indeed, much of the colonial past remains. The visitor sits on the veranda of the Singapore Cricket Club watching a match between Singapore and Penang, and thirty years drop away. The bar at the Selangor Club at Kuala Lumpur is much as it was when a quiet visiting Englishman named Maugham sat over his gin observing the skylarking of young rubber planters.

"Oh, yes, the British took a lot out of this country," Jack de Silva said in Kuala Lumpur. "But they put a lot in, too. And because they left with grace and dignity, and helped us when we needed help against Indonesia, we remember them with gratitude. Besides, anticolonialism is dead here except among the

Communists. You'd think they'd get a new slogan, wouldn't you? It doesn't impress us any more."

From Singapore and Kuala Lumpur to Laos is a long way in miles and conditions. To compare the Lion City's sophisticated economy or the energetic expansion of Malaysia with Laos is like comparing New York State with Nevada. Yet all three with Thailand make up the Southeast Asian heartland whose survival is so important to the United States. And, even in Laos, there are signs of progress.

"Laos has been backward. Laos will improve once peace is restored," says Prince Souvanna Phouma. He is right on the first point. Less than fifty Laotians were graduated in 1966 from the French-built and administered high school in Vientiane.

But Laos has certain advantages in developing an economy mainly based on rice for herself and for export. She has plenty of arable land, an advantage in populous Asia, and a well-defined program for developing it. There are no land-reform problems or population pressures in the country. The government also displays a welcome willingness to face the facts of the country's plight.

Laos's immediate requirement is rural education, enabling farmers to understand the new methods the government intends to introduce. These include better seeds, rice plants, fertilizers, pesticides, implants; the ABC's of development in much of Asia. Then comes water control—irrigation, small dams—to hold what the Mekong brings.

At present there is almost no marketing system for surplus rice, no communications. The Agricultural Development Organization, supported by the Laotian government and the United States, is building feeder roads to get the surplus rice to markets and to mills. All investment in agricultural expansion, incidentally, is from abroad; Laos is desperately short of capital, understandably so. Her tiny population supports an army larger than those of Mexico and Canada combined to fight the Pathet Lao and the North Vietnamese.

The size of the armed forces naturally has led to a shortage of manpower on the farms. Nevertheless, officials of the United States Agency for International Development office in Vientiane expect rice production to rise to 600,444 tons in the near future and then climb still higher, providing a small surplus for export. In five years Laos hopes to be exporting 200,000 tons of rice annually. Here again the ubiquitous IR-8 has appeared, with 800 tons distributed for seed. In two years there will be 40,000 more hectares available for double cropping. And, as Souvanna Phouma remarked repeatedly, "each hectare we win back and hold from the Pathet Lao goes to building the future of Laos, the peaceful future."

A visitor to Asia's frontier areas, whatever his political convictions, must be impressed by the energy, enthusiasm, and caliber of the Americans who are helping Asians develop their countries. The fervent desire to improve things, the emotional involvement with economic progress, often jeered at by Europeans, are not out of place in the hill villages and rice paddies. Of course, a traveler hears plenty of criticism from old Asia hands, particularly the French. This quite often is not directed at what the United States is doing but how it is being done: too much zeal, too much democracy with native peoples. "You Americans don't really understand these people, how they operate, what they want"; so ran the French refrain in Southeast Asia.

By the time I reached Teheran, the last stop on my long trip, I had concluded that it is the Americans who *do* understand at least what the people of Asia want. Men like Joseph Middenhall, the chief of the AID mission in Laos, Dr. Chandler of I.R.R.I., Douglas Ensminger of the Ford Foundation in India, and scores of others whose names will never make headlines, bring to their work an understanding and devotion rare under any circumstances but almost unknown to Asians of the postcolonial generation. They bear savage climates and the hazards of disease uncomplainingly. They think in terms of a future ten or twelve years hence. They may never see the results of their work. They have earned not only gratitude but respect. And they cheerfully understand that back home pundits in editorial offices and the Senate may dismiss their work as meaningless waste.

Their work sustains them. Mr. Middenhall was busy with plans for improving Laos's timber exports. Dr. Chandler travels constantly, preaching the virtues of IR-8. Mr. Ensminger looks forward to the day when India will feed herself. One day in Malaysia a young Foreign Service officer, unconsciously quoting Kipling, remarked, "It's a great work and I'm damned glad to be a part of it."

The stakes all over Asia are high. But nowhere are they higher than in Laos, Thailand, Malaysia, and Singapore. Conditions there favor independence and freedom now. The governments and peoples are responsive to United States help and eager for foreign — chiefly American — investment. Resistance to Communist expansion, either Chinese or North Vietnamese, is virile and well developed. There was in 1967 growing support for the United States intervention in Vietnam and an acute recognition of what would happen to Southeast Asia if that intervention failed or was ended as a result of a shift in American policies.

Here are governments and peoples groping toward the formation of regional groupings, welcoming the words of Japan's Foreign Minister Takeo Miki: "It is high time that not only Asia but the whole of the Asia-Pacific nations awakened to a sense of solidarity and set about cooperating in the grand task of developing Asia."

These are countries with great economic potential. They have the capacity for growth. Communist-inspired wars in Malaysia, Thailand, and Laos have weakened them to some extent, but the opportunity for development is there. These are viable societies that want to be independent and prosperous; they are worth American help.

For the remainder of this decade and into the seventies the help they need can come only from the United States. The British enjoy a great reservoir of good will throughout the area, but their resources are insufficient for the task. The French, despite much preaching by General de Gaulle about "the third world" and France's desire to help it, also lack the resources and, more important, the good will. General de Gaulle wrecked France's influence in Southeast Asia when he recognized the Communist Chinese and then journeyed to Cambodia to advise the United States to get out of Southeast Asia.

The introduction of morality into international politics is usually dangerous to the responsible government. However, Americans cannot overlook that over the years, beginning with the formation of SEATO, the United States has assumed moral obligations to the people of this area. They believe that America will help them; the whole fabric of their future would be shattered if such help were withdrawn. This may be awkward for the United States and intolerable to the neo-isolationists of the Senate and House of Representatives. Unfortunately, however, this is the way things happen to be.

V

Burmese Neutralism on the Road to Ruin

Rangoon at night conveys a sense of eerie loneliness, of an alien culture decaying in a hostile atmosphere. The visitor feels that this is what London must have been like twenty years after the legions departed. There are a few cars on the long, gently curving avenue that leads into the heart of the city, a few lights in some of the homes that now, sheltered by the velvet dark, give a false impression of opulent stability. The daylight shows the scarred stucco, the broken windows, the flapping blinds in the homes, the broken pavements of the main streets, the impressive department stores turned into slovenly government offices. A shiftless poverty is in the very air. This is Rangoon, thirty short years ago one of the most attractive and busiest cities of Asia, more prosperous than Bangkok, more comfortable than Singapore.

The capital and all Burma now are paying the price for the regime's rigid neutrality and rabid xenophobia. The economy has been in a parlous condition since 1965. The countryside is wracked by insurrection. The foundations on which Burma was built are disintegrating. Over this chaotic situation reigns the authoritarian government of General Ne Win, devoted to a Marxism it barely comprehends and seeking to inspire the people to greater effort and sacrifice with a dogma they resent and reject. The victims are the people, the placid, incurious, hospitable Burmese. As Burma's government continues its steady disengagement from the world, the people withdraw into themselves, absorbed in the minute affairs of life, the visits to the pagoda, the worship of Buddha.

From the geographical standpoint Burma's neutrality makes sense. The country's common frontier with Communist China runs for nearly thirteen hundred miles. India, the neighbor on the west, is almost overborne by staggering internal problems and threatened by China on her northern frontier. To the Burmese government, the neighbors to the east and southeast, Thailand, Malaysia, and Singapore, are committed in varying degrees to support of the United States in the contest with communism. Burma, by ceaselessly proclaiming and rigidly enforcing neutrality, can remain outside the struggle over the future of South and Southeast Asia.

Listening to Foreign Minister Thi Han and his chief permanent official, U Ohn Khin, explain and defend their policy, I felt I had heard all this before, somewhere. Of course, this was the way the Belgians, the Dutch, and the Danes talked of *their* neutrality in the turbulent months before the outbreak of World War II. They, too, believed they could avoid involvement in the war Hitler was preparing. They, too, thought that to join regional defense arrangements would enrage the aggressor and provoke invasion. They, too, believed that the aggressor had no ambitions concerning their countries.

"Our basic thinking on regional cooperation is that, if other countries sincerely want to cooperate, it is a very good thing," said Thi Han, "but conflicting interests arise out of the particular situation in which individual countries are placed and impede the development of regionalism.

"In the present context," he continued, "as far as Burma is concerned, it will be quite a while before we can enter any regional grouping, say, in the distant future.

"We favor bilateral arrangements with our neighbors and, indeed, with all countries. But as long as these countries are allied to one or another of the major powers and influenced by them, these states will not achieve real cooperation on economic and social issues in Southeast Asia. We don't condemn the Association of South East Asia, for example, but our first priority is bilateral arrangements."

For public consumption the Foreign Minister painted a happy picture of Burma's relations with China. There had "never been any pressure" along the frontier, he said. Relations with Peking had "always been good." A few days later General Ne Win remarked heatedly that he wished to God he had an atomic scissors that would cut Burma away from the mainland of Asia. Then it could be towed out to sea "away from those fellows up north," meaning the Chinese.

The official line, and that is the only side the Burmese public hears, is that the government does not condemn the United States for intervention in Vietnam because, in Thi Han's words, this "would achieve nothing in the world." Nor, of course, does it condemn North Vietnamese aggression, although the impression is that the reason for silence on this point was not the same. Here, fear is an element.

To Burma's international neutrality the government has added an interesting element: profound and wide-ranging xenophobia. The first victims of this have been the hundreds of thousands of Indians and Pakistanis who, under British rule and during the first years of Burmese independence, provided the country with administrators, businessmen, doctors and lawyers, shopkeepers. Burma, like all the countries of Southeast Asia, has a large Chinese population, but the xenophobic policy has not been applied as severely to them. The Chinese community, however, was smaller than the Indian and Pakistani and did not, the Burmese explain, present as serious a problem.

General Ne Win's government, by coercion and by encouragement, has forced between 170,000 and 180,000 Indians and Pakistanis to leave the country. In the process, one foreign diplomat said bluntly, "the government destroyed the economy of Burma by depriving it of the expertise necessary to develop its resources."

General Ne Win and his Revolutionary Council espouse an old-fashioned Marxism which they call the Burmese Way to Socialism. He and the other service officers on the council on the whole are honest and hard-working. Men of limited outlook and no experience in industry or commerce, they considered Marxism the ideal way to run a country. They also hotly resented the domination of Burma's economy by the Indians, Pakistanis, and Chinese. They were, and are, nationalists, and they saw Marxism and the expulsion of the foreigners as the means of consolidating control of the country in their hands.

The instrument of control is now the army. Even if Burma was at peace internally, which she is not, the ability of an untrained officer corps to deal with her problems would be doubtful. But Burma's government is fighting at least five insurrections. General Ne Win admits that his regime controls only 65 per cent of the country, and Communist bands within the last few years have penetrated to the outskirts of Rangoon.

Under these conditions an army colonel may find himself saddled with three jobs; one I met had four. But it is more usual to encounter a colonel, for example, who at the same time commands a battalion theoretically in action against rebels, administers a district where communications are haphazard and the people indifferent, and runs some important enterprise like a rice mill. He is suited, again in theory, only for the first. And, with the departure of the foreigners, there is no one of experience to help or advise.

The result is that the country's infant industries—all nationalized—the railroads, the distribution system for consumer goods, the collection of rice and its milling are in a chaotic state.

One set of statistics symbolizes Burma's economic malaise. In the past she was one of the great rice-exporting countries of Asia, selling 1,600,000 tons abroad in 1962. In 1967 the most optimistic estimate was that rice exports would be around 600,000 tons, with other estimates as low as 400,000 tons. Rice is Burma's leading earner of foreign exchange and, as a result in the decline in exports, the country cannot import the consumer goods, particularly textiles, that it needs.

One evening in Maymyo, the hill town that was Burma's summer capital during British rule, I met a friendly Burmese walking in the botanical gardens that the British left behind.

In the old days, he said, before Ne Win, he had been able to buy perhaps three longyis, the wrap-around skirt worn by both men and women, each year. Now he was lucky if he had the money to buy one.

"My wife has to wait in line at the state shops, sometimes for five hours, for everything. When she finally gets to the counter, the things she wants are gone. And even if they are there, she has to pay sixty per cent more than she did in the old days.

"We have a joke now," he said. "The government has nationalized the leprosariums. So we say, fine, soon there will be no more leprosy. You see, once anything is nationalized it disappears."

Why has rice production fallen? Largely because of the lack of incentive. Some farmers withhold their rice because the government price is too low. Others sell it on the black market where the higher prices enable them to buy consumer goods. Still others turn to raising poultry and bananas, certain that these can always be sold on the black market. The government has responded by imposing jail sentences of up to three years on recalcitrant farmers, but to no avail. Rice is not flowing into the mills. Nor is it likely to until the government alters its present policy and reintroduces incentives and efficiency into the economy.

To those who wish the Burmese well, the situation is tragic.

The land is fertile; no one is starving in Burma. The birth rate is not terribly high; there is less population pressure than anywhere in Southeast Asia except in Laos and Cambodia. There is plenty of land for all.

Elsewhere in Asia these conditions could be changed by foreign technological aid and financial assistance. But the Burmese government, in the words of one experienced foreign diplomat, "are like a lot of damned old ladies about aid."

Some financial assistance still comes to Burma, the residue of past credits. But General Ne Win, pursuing neutrality, doesn't like foreign aid, fearing it will give foreigners—the word has the connotation of enemies in Burma—too much influence in the country. In extremis, the Burmese will accept help from small countries and from the Japanese. They believe the Japanese, who ruled the country with heavy hand from 1942 to 1945, owe it to them.

(One of the more ludicrous bits of Ne Win's mythology, one that is accepted by the Burmese, is that the country liberated itself from the Japanese. What happened is that the Burmese army, which had industriously cooperated with the invaders, saw what was happening and deserted the occupiers for the new invaders, the British armies coming down from the north.)

"Let me tell you how the Burmese feel about aid," a diplomat said. "If the United States offered to loan them one hundred million dollars and to send ten technicians to supervise its expenditure, they'd refuse the offer. Those ten technicians spell foreign influence. The Chinese gave them a whacking big loan. They wouldn't draw on it. The Chinese had to send Chou En-lai down here to say that Burma's refusal to draw on the loan was an affront to China. *Then* they drew on it, all right. Mustn't offend the Chinese. But generally they don't want to take anything from any major power."

Burma in the late spring of 1967, in the view of most foreign diplomats in Rangoon, was on the edge of change. But change in Asia is never rapid, and it was doubtful whether the Burmese government had yet understood the gravity of the economic situation. For General Ne Win's response to the crisis seemed feeble, indeed. It consisted in bringing into Rangoon, from all over Burma, the leading workers in Burma's agriculture and industry. Once in the capital, these budding Burmese Stakhanovites were subjected to a series of lectures intended to spur them to still further efforts on behalf of the Burmese Way to Socialism. The atmosphere at the old British race course, where the gathering was held, was half way between a low-grade revival meeting and an amusement park. In many Asian countries the visitor is struck by how much has been done against great odds since independence. In Burma the reverse is true: the visitor is shocked to see how far the country has gone downhill.

The government's inability to deal effectively with the economy is due to a great degree with its preoccupation with the various guerrilla wars that plague the country. For a decade fighting has flickered across the great silent hills of the north and east and flared in placid villages of the Irrawaddy delta. In 1962 the Union of Burma was on the verge of breaking up into separate states. Ne Win has averted that but at considerable cost. Burma has 165,000 troops and police in the field fighting insurgency. They are doing no more than holding their own against the insurgents. Wherever one looks in Burma there is trouble.

In the far north of the country the Kachins are in the field. In the east the Karens raid into the delta. The Shans, in east-central Burma, are on the warpath. In the Irrawaddy delta two Communist guerrilla forces, the White Flags and the Red Flags, prey on the farmers and the villages. Burma is about the size of Texas, and when the planes stop at little airfields in the hills the atmosphere must resemble that of our own frontier a century ago. Some tribes are "up," meaning they are fighting; others are "restive," including the Nagas, the Chins, and the Mons, the visitor is told.

"The country has not known unity since Independence, and it is divided politically, economically, socially, and racially," General Ne Win has said. "The task of leading the country now is like having to lead an army in disarray, and it is a very onerous one, requiring all of one's energy, thought, and action for rebuilding the broken fabric of unity."

True enough as far as it goes. What the General omitted is that this confused situation in Burma offers the Chinese a multiplicity of choices. By infiltrating, arming, and directing any one or any combination of the insurgent groups, they can insure the disruption of the Union of Burma. Or by the development of a pro-Peking faction within Burmese socialism, they can gradually swing the Ne Win government into neutrality against the rest of independent Asia and for Chinese communism.

This second process seemed in 1967 to be in full swing. Chinese influence, although restrained in its expression, was growing in the dominant party, among intellectuals, and in the schools and universities. There were echoes from Peking in newspaper editorials. The prevailing xenophobia did not apparently apply to the Chinese as long as they worked quietly for their own interests. China, incidentally, regards Burma as former Chinese territory "seized by the British imperialists." General Ne Win knows this. He is aware of China's ambitions. But while his government pursues neutrality, there is very little that he can do about it.

The dead hopelessness of Burma's situation occasionally is lit by a gleam of national character that shows an inner determination usually obscured by the Burmese outer placidity. Flying north I talked to an engineer about the trials of his profession in a chaotic country. He gestured toward the distant hills.

"Three months to build a bridge up there and some insurgents blew it up in three minutes," he said bitterly.

He showed me a long white scar on his forearm. "I got that when they jumped us," he said. "But we go on. This insurgency is taking all the government's money and soldiers who should be in the labor force. But we go on."

One of General Ne Win's colonels was on the plane. When he departed from Taung-gyi airfield, which is in the heart of "insurgent country," he was escorted by at least a company of infantry. Riflemen surrounded the tiny airport building. There was an air of nervous excitement. The stop was the shortest I experienced in Asia.

The Shans, Karens, and Kachins never have identified themselves with the Burmese state. Under British rule these tough hillmen were kept happy by employment as irregular troops under British officers. Then as now they looked down on the pacific Burmese of the plains. Their political goals are half formed and constantly changing. Sometimes they demand the establishment of independent states; this is especially true of the Karens. The Shans and the Kachins favor local autonomy for Shan and Kachin states within the Union of Burma. When the Rangoon government tells them that in the Union all races can and should work together, the insurgents make rude noises and run off some livestock and women.

The insurgents' numbers are not large. The Karen National Defense Organization claims that the "state" is defended by an army of 5,200. The Shan forces are about 3,800 strong, but very well armed. In Shan State east of the Salween River, the Shans grow poppies and make opium. The opium goes south on mule-back into Thailand—trains of as many as a thousand mules have been seen—where the opium is exchanged for money and arms. The Kachin forces in the north number about 2,300.

In Rangoon the Foreign Minister spoke darkly of "mis-

sionaries" who had encouraged the insurgents. The Karens are
Baptists, and there are Baptists and Catholics among the Kachins. But the religious and ideological context of the insurgency
seems limited among these tribes.

"We just don't like these Burmese," a Shan farmer said in
the market at Maymyo. "We want to be independent of them."

The country favors the insurgents. The forested hills offer
cover for raiding parties and strongholds against government
reprisal. The roads are poor and winding, providing innumerable
opportunities for ambush. The government troops toiling
through the mist-shrouded mountains are harried and sniped at as
they move from town to town. Of course much of the insurgency, although dignified as a fight for independence, is only a
return to the dacoitry that has plagued Burma for hundreds of
years. The Ne Win government is learning what Kipling's Private
Mulvaney learned in the eighties of the last century, that without
his gun and his knife, the dacoit—or insurgent—is a peaceful
farmer and "a felony for to shoot."

A hard-working captain of the People's Police Force gave the
impression that counterinsurgency operations are a difficult way
to make a living. Not long ago, he said, the Karens had run off
four cows and two women and burned a village in his territory.
After a ten-day pursuit, he was ambushed by the Karens. After
a brief fight he parleyed. The Karens were honest with him. They
were sorry the village had been burned, for it was a favorite of
theirs. The cows had been butchered. As for the women, they
liked life with the insurgents and wouldn't return home for
anything.

"Now, how am I to put that in an official report?" he asked.

Of the two Communist groups in the delta the White Flags,
whose strength is estimated at about three thousand men, are
more important. They are operating in the richest agricultural
land in Burma and they are encouraged by the Communist

Chinese, although there was no evidence that this encouragement now extends to anything more tangible than exhortations to fight harder. Although vigorous government action has reduced their numbers—there were fifteen thousand White Flags in 1948—these insurgents are still troublesome, especially in view of Burma's parlous economic situation. One of their tactics is to terrorize peasants who sell rice to the government. The usual method is to kill the peasant by slitting open his belly and stuffing the wound with rice. Not a pretty sight.

The thousand or so Red Flags practice an extremist communism that considers even Peking's brand too mild. They operate in the same areas of the delta as about five hundred religious fanatics with whom they frequently clash.

Burma's inability to put down the insurgency is not due basically to a lack of force or even to the perplexing problem of supplying troops in bad terrain. The army musters ninety-nine infantry battalions, a tank battalion, two armored-car battalions, and four artillery battalions. The air force's forty-four helicopters, if properly employed, should be able to provide the necessary support for the company- or battalion-sized actions that the army throws at the insurgents. The essential difficulty is that Burma's natural soldiers and fighters are all on the insurgents' side.

The overwhelming first impression of Burma in Rangoon is that of an underdeveloped country hard pressed in the struggle for survival. This impression is sharpened by the huge billboards and posters in the Communist style—brawny workers marching shoulder to shoulder with the army and the like—that adorn the streets and by the strident exhortations to greater productivity that pour from the radio and fill the newspapers. But as the days pass the visitor catches fleeting glimpses of another Burma, an older Burma that is not at all interested in General Ne Win or the Burmese Way to Socialism or more tons of rice and yards of textile. Burma is a country with a dual personality. And once the visitor leaves Rangoon he finds the second Burma predominant.

The Fokker Friendship stops first at Taung-gyi's Heho airport. Then it makes two further stops in the uplands. There is less danger here, and the crew and passengers gossip as freight is unloaded. Then, finally, the plane drifts down across a bare, baked plain, a broad river, and the pagodas and palaces of Mandalay. This old capital from which Burma's kings ruled has an antique, faded dignity. Whatever may be happening in Rangoon, whoever may be ruling, Mandalay says, this is Burma.

Of all the pagodas none is more striking than Mandalay's Arakan pagoda, so called because the great gold Buddha about which it is built was hauled over the mountains from Arakan on the coast of the Bay of Bengal. Over the centuries the gifts of the pious have covered the idol with gold to a depth of many inches. The faces of those praying near the Buddha have a remote placidity. All the clamorous life of Asia now is hushed in this small square before the great gold figure.

But the Arakan pagoda, like European churches in the Middle Ages, is also a place of business. Toy shops, curio shops, jewelry shops line the passages that lead to the Buddha. There is a friendly, relaxed air; worshipers pause to gossip, thankful to be out of the blistering sunlight. An old man sleeps on the cool tiles behind the Buddha. In the pagoda time *does* stand still.

The road past Mandalay to Maymyo, the old summer capital, winds across the Irrawaddy plain and then abruptly begins to climb. At three thousand feet the heavy heat of the lowlands drops away, and, pausing, the traveler can see Mandalay in the distance, lying beside the broad silver ribbon of the Irrawaddy. From that distance the city looks much as it might when King Thebaw ruled and Victoria's troops were a menace more distant than the Chinese are today.

If Mandalay is a reminder of Burma's royal past, Maymyo

stands as memorial to that later empire that conquered King Thibaw's Burma and now itself lies shattered. The English who built Maymyo made a touching attempt to recall their homes half a world away. Here are Tudor cottages and Victorian manor houses. Their names, neatly painted on the gateposts, are fading now: Balmoral and Oakwood and Pine Lodge. The driveways are overgrown and the houses themselves, now tenanted by Burmese, have an unhappy air of neglect. But how gay it must have been a half century ago when the carriages circled through the town and young subalterns played tennis in the long afternoons with girls fresh from home! The English have gone now. But they left behind a small colony of retired Ghurkhas who farm outside Maymyo and view the Burmese with contempt.

"We came here during the fighting in nineteen forty-five and saw that the land was good," said one ex-havildar (sergeant). "So when my service was over I returned. We raise fruit and vegetables for the market. No, the Burmese have not attacked us as foreigners." I got the impression he half hoped they would. "They are children in a man's world. These Shans for instance." He swept his arm toward the green mountain wall of the Shan hills. "One company—no, half a company—of my regiment and we would teach them to behave."

There were plenty of Shans in the Maymyo market the next morning: small, wiry men with blue tattooing on their arms. The Burmese, I noticed, eyed them warily. For although individual Burmese are capable of sudden, mad gusts of rage, they are not a violent or a militant people. From what I heard from these and other Burmese, there probably would be no outrageous outcry if General Ne Win were to allow the Shans, the Karens, and the Kachins to set up independent states, providing this left Burma in peace.

The Burma that the world sees is not in fact the Burma that its people love. The world is presented with a country gripped by major economic difficulties arising from nationalization, the eviction of foreigners, and the incompetence of the army officers; what a Marxist might call the unintended consequences of socialist action. This same country is harassed and occasionally humiliated by small bands of tribesmen whose activities impose a heavy burden in manpower and money upon the government. Finally the Burmese are subjected to all the phony propaganda claptrap of a Marxist authoritarian government. No people are less suited to it.

Neutrality and xenophobia—the latter, as I have shown, a perverted form of nationalism—are the mainsprings of government policy. But the friendly, talkative Burmese are following their own policy, which amounts to withdrawal from the world. Their wants are simple: a new longyi, enough fat for cooking, rice, time to gossip and go to the pagoda. They are highly unsophisticated and not materialistic. In the countryside they are superstitious. There, although they are faithful followers of the way of the Lord Buddha, the traveler sees along the roadsides tiny shrines filled with offerings to propitiate the nats or evil spirits.

The Burmese government's errors of omission and commission would excite a rebellion among less placid folk. But although there is plenty of grumbling, no one sees any wisdom in action. Rather, they enjoy a quiet withdrawal from both the world that rumbles and strives around Burma's frontiers and from active participation in their own destinies.

On the plane from Mandalay to Rangoon I sat next to a young Burmese who tried, patiently, to explain to this materialistic Westerner what he wanted out of life. It was simply to "live as we have always lived, to follow the Lord Buddha, to be at peace with ourselves. We can never be a strong country. But we may find a kind of peace in our very weakness. You Americans can't understand that, can you?"

This attitude really is the greatest obstacle to General Ne Win's plans to refashion Burma into a socialist state. The government works hard, if at times with appalling inefficiency, and is not notably corrupt. The General and his associates recognize the weakness of the economy, but they are eternally talking about the need for time. Come in ten years, the visitor is told; then you will see what we have done for Burma.

What must be done as soon as possible, in the opinion of worried foreign diplomats, is the decontrol of the internal distribution of rice and of the distribution of consumer goods. The government, which jealously guards its overseas credits, must spend some to create a mild inflation that will give the people more spending money. Will the government take steps that deny the wisdom of all it has done since taking power? Most foreigners in Rangoon doubt it.

Compared to her colossal neighbor to the west, India, and to the vital, progressing states to the east and southeast, Burma today is a backwater. But no Asian can overlook that Burma was in the past and could be again a leading exporter of rice, the grain that Asia needs. Similarly, in all the capitals of the area, officials and military men look worriedly at the map and point to Burma. If the Chinese should ever come *that* way, through Burma, they say, or use the insurgents to start a War of National Liberation, communism would reach the Indian Ocean and southern Asia would be cut in half. This has not happened yet. But that is no reason to think it cannot happen.

The nights in Rangoon, while not cool, are less oppressive than the days. But even then it is a depressing city. The solitary stroller must keep his eyes on the pavement to avoid the broken pavings. When he does look up he sees fine buildings, once the headquarters of foreign banks, now housing government departments where hundreds of clerks listlessly pass paper from one desk to another. The curse of Asian education is the concentration on turning out lawyers and civil servants rather than farmers and engineers. Nowhere is it more pronounced than in Burma. There is one agricultural college at Pyinmana and, when the government gets around it, a second may be established at Prome.

Now, at night, the street stalls are busy. Their wares are pitiful: a few badly rolled cheroots, tins of pipe tobacco, cigarette lighters for which there is no fuel, cakes iced in nauseous colors. Beyond the flare of the lanterns that light the stalls, the poor of Rangoon are settling for the night on pavements still warm from the day's sun.

The lights of the hotel shine on deserted streets. The hotel is so quiet that in the lobby the solitary visitor can hear two waiters chatting in the bar fifty yards away. It is a big hotel and was, in the old days, a gay one. Businessmen met in the bar and young officers flirted in the lofty, airy cocktail lounge. Now tiny bugs emerge from the cane chairs and bite the unwary.

The only other visitor was an Indian from Calcutta who had returned to Rangoon to complete the liquidation of his clothing business. He was interested to learn I was on my way to India. He didn't know whether I would like it, but "there at least you will find we are alive."

VI

The Indian Question Mark

The two stout pillars of independence in Asia are Japan on the east and India on the west. Between them, in a great arc that runs from the Philippines to Burma, lie the smaller states struggling to reinforce their political and economic stability. They number many millions. But the states are not powerful enough or advanced enough to balance the enormous weight of Communist China unless they are tied to Japan and India. No counterpoise to China's weight can be established without the full cooperation of these two countries. Japan, as we have seen, is already moving, albeit rather slowly, toward that role in the east. India is the question mark.

The American difficulty is that, if the United States intends to support independence and freedom in Asia, a viable India in the west is a prerequisite. But this enormous state with a population closing in on 520 million is the most vulnerable of the great independent Asian powers. Her unity is threatened by separatist movements. The economy—indeed, the entire society —is recovering slowly from the disaster of two successive failures of the monsoon. In the north fourteen Chinese divisions, and, more important, the danger of Wars of National Liberation fomented by China in the small states along the northern frontier, pose a constant threat to India. Finally there is the old, bitter quarrel with Pakistan over Kashmir, a quarrel now exacerbated by China's active support for the Pakistanis.

India's preoccupation with China and her huge internal difficulties have forced her to look to the north and the northeast. This is a profound disadvantage at a time when any effective policy to offset Chinese strength calls for closer ties between India and the countries to the southeast. Another difficulty is that too many Indian politicians, officials, and intellectual leaders still remain enamored of the role they assumed under Jawaharlal Nehru, that of leader of the Afro-Asian nations. Nowadays only the Indians appear to take this role seriously, rejoicing in their position as an international nanny breathing self-righteousness and exuding advice. Southeast Asia would benefit if India were to pay more attention to the problems of that area and spend less time in lecturing the world at large.

Shifting India's attention from the north and from her supposed position as the leader of the third world to a more realistic role as the ally and supporter of the nations to the southeast appears, then, to be one of the more important operations for United States diplomacy. The attempt to do so must be made, and made despite the knowledge that India herself is not now the strongest anchor for such a grouping, that she could under certain circumstances break up overnight. But the United States has no option. If there is to be coherent support for independent states vs. communism, India must be supported. The United States must work with the tools at hand.

A viable India, the India of Nehru's dreams, strong, self-sufficient, proud; how far away that seems. For nearly twenty years American liberals have taken the dream for the fact. The fact is that India is in a desperate situation, one that encourages pessimism. The teeming, hungry millions in Calcutta. The harsh, baked plains of central India. The immensity of every problem facing the government. The enormous gap between rich and poor in a society supposedly seeking socialism. The corruption that extends from the highest level to the office boy who must be bribed to carry a file from one desk to another in a government office.

Yet, when the visitor leaves, he does so with a sense of awe. These people can stand so much: famine and natural disaster, wars and riots, colossal governmental blundering. India takes the buffets fate gives her, shakes her head, and groggily stumbles forward. In the mass, India is heroic.

The condition of India, her ability to play a constructive role in Asia, hang on the outcome of one overriding problem: the food-population equation. Raising enough food to feed an increasing population is a problem in most Asian countries. Nowhere is it more acute than in India. A single statistic emphasizes the problem. There are over 520 million Indians, at least 150 million more than there were twenty years ago. Thus India's population has been augmented in two decades by as many people as there were in the United States in 1950.

The control of population growth and the expansion of agricultural productivity consequently are the two most important programs facing the Indian government.

Dr. Sripati Chandrasekhar, the Minister of Health and Family Planning, is one of the most forceful and intelligent public officials I encountered in Asia. His difficulty, not unknown elsewhere on the continent, is that plans and projects hatched in the capital must be carried out in the field in the face of staggering administrative inefficiency.

"Here is the situation," he said briskly. "In population we are well past the five-hundred-million mark, probably around five hundred and twenty million. We have twenty million births a year, eight million deaths. We add twelve million to the population every year. At this rate there will be a billion Indians by the year two thousand. Remember, that's only thirty-three years away. Even now, after two monsoon failures, there are ten million people literally on the verge of starvation. Something *must* be done."

Dr. Chandrasekhar sees vasectomy, male sterilization, as the most promising approach. The operation is quick, leaves the man able to enjoy intercourse, and has, he claimed, a great psychological advantage. Men, the Minister explained, understand and want to solve India's great problem. Perhaps; the arrival of a government jeep bearing a sterilization team in a village quite often starts an exodus of all males to the nearest hiding places.

The loop, the intrauterine contraceptive device, has proved only 70 per cent effective in India, he said, although 800,000 were inserted in 1965. Ten per cent of the loops drop out, another 10 per cent are taken out because they cause bleeding, and the third 10 per cent are removed because of discomfort. The introduction of the contraceptive pill, Dr. Chandrasekhar said, is a long-term program. At present it is used by educated, sophisticated women in India's cities but not in the 560,000 villages in which 80 per cent of Indians live. The government has asked the United States Agency for International Development for one million dollars' worth of pills as a free grant. These pills are to be used as an experimental measure from the end of 1967. Meanwhile India is planning the construction of plants to manufacture the pill.

"We have no dogmatic approach to any contraceptive," he said. "We'll do anything, anything. Ask the man to sleep on the roof, if that helps."

The government program inevitably has encountered resistance in a traditional society. Dr. Chandrasekhar wants to raise the age of consent from sixteen to twenty years and has prodded the government to prepare legislation to this end. This has affronted Hindu traditionalists and many of India's 30 million Moslems. The measure, he said, will "save about one baby in each marriage," because a girl marrying at twenty will have a shorter span of childbearing than one marrying at sixteen. The government also is carrying out a widespread propaganda campaign aimed at inducing couples to limit their families to three. Finally, in view of the economic and social pressures imposed by the rising birth rate, the government intends to liberalize the law against abortion.

To such an enthusiast even the massive job of reaching India's villages is manageable. At present teams of surgeons, male and female, visit the villages by jeep. There they gather the people, explain their purpose, and perform vasectomies. But progress is painfully slow. The team, even if it limits its stay in a single village to one hour, is able to visit only four or five villages a day.

"We need helicopters, lots of them," the Minister said. "Give us time and we'll cut the birth rate still further. Why, already we've reduced it from forty in one thousand to twenty or twenty-five in one thousand."

Every effort is being made to encourage men to accept sterilization. The man receives forty rupees from the government and, if he is a government servant, five days' leave. India's major industries have been induced to spread propaganda for population control.

Obstacles abound. There are not enough women doctors to insert loops; the Minister estimated that India needs another twelve thousand. There are not enough condoms available; the present supply of a million a month is insufficient. More are being bought abroad, chiefly in Japan. American prices are too high. Finally, of course, there is what the Minister called "the sense of apathy" in the villages.

"The President, the Prime Minister, and the Deputy Prime Minister are one hundred per cent behind me," Dr. Chandrasekhar said. "On the whole I am most optimistic. The job will be done. There is no doubt about that. Why, we're finding new methods every day. Family planning units in the factories. Propaganda to the twelve million industrial workers, a captive audience. There's a family planning unit in every government ministry."

Such enthusiasm is infectious. But it should be remembered that India is just beginning to tackle the problem and that enthusiasm and drive at the top do not always penetrate to lower echelons. The Ministry, aside from its jeep teams, at the outset had no national organization to implement its plans, and the programs in the Indian states varied in effectiveness. Those in Mysore, Bengal, Gujarat, and the Punjab, were considered as good. Elsewhere the states have not understood the urgency of the problem.

The change in attitude toward population control at the top, of course, is a great advantage because it has made possible the propaganda drive that is slowly impressing the country. But because the government still does not appear to understand the application of modern administrative measures to the problem, progress lags. The real limits to the program are physical, logistical: the scarcity of doctors, especially women doctors; the failure of any propaganda program, no matter how extensive, to reach more than a fraction of India's illiterate millions; the shortages of pills, loops, condoms, and other contraceptive devices.

"They've got to put in a crash program, that's all there is to it," an American expert said. "The future of India is at stake. They'll have to end this business of using existing machinery in the states and develop their own in the central government. Of course, the conservative element doesn't want this. They'll have to get over that. Do you realize there are more people in India than in Africa and South America together?"

United States interest in this primary problem and willingness to help was expressed by a gift of $1,300,000 to India to buy contraceptives in the United States and distribute them through commercial channels. The Agency for International Development announced late in 1967 that $800,000 will go to supply 100 million contraceptives for males and the remaining

$500,000 for birth control pills for 100,000 Indian women who are to test them over a period of a year and a half.

The gift marked a shift in American policy on assistance in population control problems. As late as 1959 President Eisenhower said that it was "not a proper political or governmental activity or function or responsibility."

Since then successive administrations have been forced to change their attitudes by the emergence of the population problem as the most serious issue facing many governments. To supplement the direct aid to India, the United States also is increasing its subsidy to the International Planned Parenthood Federation by $2,500,000. Of this total, $1,000,000 will be used to purchase American commodities, including contraceptives, and the rest for training programs in India, Pakistan, and Turkey as well as in Latin America and East Asia.

The United States venture in India, its first substantial assistance to a foreign country's family planning program, is part of the effort made to meet one side of the problem in India. The other side of the problem is food. Here again we see circumstances forcing a drastic change in Indian thinking about economic priorities.

It took the Indian government twenty years to recognize that the emphasis in national planning and development should be placed on agriculture, specifically on food crops. This is almost incredible in a country in which food has been a continuing crisis for centuries; there were twelve famines between 1765 and 1858. Nevertheless, Indian politicos and members of the Planning Commission havered over priorities. The first Five-Year Plan (1951–56) gave priority to agriculture. Then the weight shifted in succeeding plans to industry. Prime Minister Nehru and his followers were convinced that India must be industrialized if she were to be a significant and independent world power.

The inadequacy of the agricultural development program in the late fifties and early sixties had had an effect on food production even before the monsoon failures in 1965 and 1966 struck India. Rice output alone dropped by eight million tons in each of these two years.

The Indian government can produce impressive statistics showing over-all improvements in the fifties and early sixties. The net acreage sown rose from 293 million acres to 334 million; the total cropped area from 325 million to 384 million. The gross area irrigated rose by nearly 20 per cent. It was good but it was not enough. The weakness of these government statistics is that they stress the increase in acreage cultivated rather than on increasing yields per acre in land already farmed. Agricultural technology throughout Asia has demonstrated that more intensive farming, doubling and sometimes tripling acreage yields, is the best answer to the rising demands for food.

The current Five-Year Plan calls for an annual production of 125 million tons of food grains by the end of 1971, the last year of the plan. This means an increase of nearly 40 million tons over the figures for 1965. (Incidentally, the population of India is expected to be about 550 million in 1971.) Can India reach this ambitious target?

Foreign experts who are not politically involved with governmental planning are doubtful. Douglas Ensminger of the Ford Foundation thought it "well within the realm of possibility" that India could meet most of her food needs by 1977.

The failure of two monsoons and one winter rain set back Indian agriculture by two, possibly three, years. Mr. Ensminger thought that by 1972 there would be a "sense of real progress in agriculture." There are great possibilities. The 120,000 square miles of the Ganges basin and the 40,000 square miles of the Indus basin should be able to feed India and, in time, produce food for export. But solid progress will depend almost as much on the willingness of the Indian farmer to absorb and apply modern agricultural methods as it will on adequate rainfall.

Until now, the main causes of what even government officials admit is an indifferent record in agricultural production have been a shortage of modern fertilizers, unrealistic, vaguely socialist land policies that restrict the size of farms, and the absence of incentives to the farmers. The government is moving now to apply agricultural technology in the villages, introducing new strains of rice and wheat, improving irrigation through a newly appointed Irrigation Commission, and teaching the farmers to use fertilizers, pesticides, and new implements.

The shortage of fertilizers has been and will be for some time a critical element of the food crisis. One estimate is that a judicious use of chemical fertilizers would raise crop production by 70 million tons. But obtaining the fertilizer raises a problem. The construction of fertilizer plants requires a great deal of money, much of it in foreign exchange. If India is to provide her farms with the chemical fertilizers they need, expenditure must be diverted from industrial development. She cannot, in her present state, do both.

Resistance to modernization by farmers is common throughout Asia, but in many countries, certainly much of India, reports have been exaggerated. Farmers, especially in north India, despite limited funds, are absorbing new techniques and buying, when they can, new implements. The restriction on land holdings is an impediment. The ceilings on land holdings, fixed by state law, are usually around thirty acres. This is a barrier to large-scale farming, and critical Indians told me that in some states, especially the Punjab, thousands of acres of food land go untilled because of the restrictions.

"The farmer wants more land, he wants to do better, he'll experiment with any new strain of wheat or rice available," according to an official of the Agency for Industrial Development. "Traditionalism is going under because the inducements of a cash crop are now so obvious. Self-sufficient by nineteen seventy-one? That's too much to ask of India. But agriculture is better placed now than it was a few years ago to reach that goal. And don't, for God's sake, think that the Indians, farmers or officials, *like* getting food from the United States."

Whether the Indians like it or not, they get a great deal of food from America under Public Law 480. Under this law American food grains sold in India are paid for by rupees. All food aid from the West has been running at between 8 and 10 per cent of India's annual food requirements. Of course, as sensitive Indians point out, they are not the only Asian country buying food abroad. The Chinese in 1965 concluded one of the largest wheat purchases in history, buying 223,800,000 bushels from Canada for 403 million dollars.

No assessment of the future of India's struggle to feed herself can discount the importance of regular rainfall even if present plans for irrigation and water storage are completely fulfilled. This is what rain meant to India in one year: Rainfall over the crop year from July 1965 to June 1966 was 12.5 per cent below normal. Total output of food grains fell by 18 per cent. But in 1964–65, when the rainfall was above normal, India raised a record food crop of 89 million tons, or 8 per cent higher than the previous best output.

In view of the towering importance of the food-population equation, the stress laid on industrial development in India strikes a visitor as almost immaterial except where, as in food-processing industries, it bears on the central problem. Yet, in New Delhi, officials appeared as concerned over the slump in industrial development in 1966 and early 1967 as they did over the appalling prospect of famine. The industrial decline, naturally, was connected with the farm crisis. The latter necessitated the import of large amounts of food and fertilizer and consequently led to restrictions on foreign exchange allocations for industrial raw materials. The situation was exacerbated by the war with Pakistan over Kashmir in the autumn of 1965, a war, incidentally, whose political and economic repercussions have been far more lasting and serious in Southern Asia than the West recognizes.

The war led to the temporary suspension of United States aid at a time when India had to meet demands for war production. Industry was asked to get along with a third of the normal amount of imported raw materials. With resources diverted to defense and to averting famine, the government was forced to reduce spending on industrial development. This affected the entire industrial economy. Steel consumption fell, construction dwindled, private investment slowed down.

When a nation is overtaken by an economic malaise, a government concentrates on consolidation rather than expansion. This is what has been happening in India since 1966. This trend is likely to continue as long as the effects of the food crisis impose a drain on the economy. Most foreign experts agree that what India requires during the period of the present Five-Year Plan is continued and expanded emphasis on agricultural production, the raising of existing industries to full capacity, and the development only of those industries necessary to the country's defense. To this most Indian conservatives would add an end to the present complex tax structure and to the government controls, which they believe have reduced initiative and enterprise.

Drawing a balance sheet for India after twenty years of independence would be too long and too complex for this short book. But because a viable, independent India is essential to stability in Asia, some assessment should be attempted if only in the area of national direction and morale.

India's leaders, customarily more attracted to grandiose

political ideas than to the hard facts of economics, after two decades of trial have had to face the unwelcome thought that India has not done as well as her founders expected. Sympathetic foreigners like United States Ambassador Chester Bowles can recite India's accomplishments—and they make good reading: an increase of 700 per cent in steel production, a rise in electric power capacity to five times what it was in 1953 with the expectation it will double again in five years, the reduction of malaria from 100,000,000 cases annually to less than 50,000 in 1966, the doubling of general industrial output, a rise in life expectancy by eighteen years. All these are solid achievements. But they must be seen in the perspective of what this enormous, harsh country demands. India has made great progress. India has not conquered her economic, social, and political problems; she is not a world criterion for social democracy. And it is too late now to blame the British.

Listening to Prime Minister Indira Gandhi and other cabinet ministers, it was clear that India's recent tribulations have promoted a new mood of self-criticism and self-examination that is a more hopeful psychological approach to progress than the complacency of the past. It is not only that the agricultural and other economic problems are recognized in their ghastly magnitude. The government is keenly aware that a combination of circumstances—the decline in the prestige and political power of the Congress Party, strikingly evident in its sorry showing in the 1967 elections, the absence of a coherent, responsible opposition, the strain imposed on the economy by the 1965 war and rising defense needs—have encouraged forces that threaten the dissolution of the Indian Union.

A menacing factor, often discounted in the West, is the opportunity which the present situation offers powerful elements in the Communist Party that are vehemently pro-Peking in the ideological struggle between the Russian and the Chinese parties. In West Bengal, where poverty and political instability seem to be worst, the state government is an incoherent united front of fourteen parties in which the left-wing, or pro-Peking, Communists are the dominant force. Under this government the number of *gheraos,* a form of coercion by labor in which members of the management of a factory are surrounded and denied freedom of movement, has been on the increase. Sharecroppers have begun to forcibly occupy and till the holdings of big landlords. Both industrial workers and sharecroppers had grievances. But both were goaded to extreme measures by the left-wing Communists, who claim more than 75 per cent of union membership. All this in a state that boasts most of India's heavy industry. Naturally, new investment is at a standstill.

No one can even glimpse the poverty and misery of Calcutta's back streets without feeling that something must be done. No one can talk to representatives of the left-wing Communists, or the highly radical pro-Mao Tse-tung fringe, without being convinced that these are not the people to do it. Idealistic, impractical, yet greedy for power, they are the heralds of chaos. Given a weak central government in New Delhi they can speed the process of disintegration that now menaces India's unity.

The growing strength of the pro-Peking Communists surprises outsiders when they consider China's successful seizure of Indian territory in Ladakh during the 1962 clash, Peking's menacing gestures during the Kashmir fighting in 1965, the intermittent forays across India's northern frontier from Kashmir to Assam, and the Communists' support, political and military, of Pakistan in its quarrel with India over Kashmir.

One reason for these Communists' new strength is the appeal of one of their basic arguments to many Indians. Faced with the supposedly enormous military strength of China, there is a tendency, especially among some Indian intellectuals, to think in terms of appeasement rather than resolute national defense. This is an attitude tailor-made for acquiescence to the Chinese assertion that with good will and understanding on both sides all issues between the two governments can be resolved. The United States and the Soviet Union are portrayed by Peking as too involved in their own cooperation to risk real help in India in a crisis. The logic of the situation, the Communists proclaim, calls for a détente, one that can be obtained by India, if it follows the ideas of the pro-Peking faction. The Chinese dragon is perfectly willing to be housebroken—as long as the dragon dominates the Indian house.

In those Indian states where the pro-Peking wing of the Communist Party is strong, there is another, less ambitious argument. This is that the breakup of the Indian Union is the only path to economic health for the state concerned. Here again Peking is pursuing its main objective, albeit by more parochial means. This is the ultimate destruction of democratic India as an independent, democratic state with the potential of balancing China as a great power in Asia.

Finally, all Chinese Communist policy toward India, either as it is practiced by the Foreign Ministry in Peking or by Communist politicians in India, is now connected directly to the twenty-year-old quarrel with Pakistan over Kashmir, a quarrel that infects every aspect of Indian international relations. This quarrel itself is part of the complex of problems India faces on her northern frontiers.

As far as the peace of Asia is concerned, Kashmir is as dangerous an issue as the question of Alsace and Lorraine was to Europe's peace at the turn of the century.

The genesis of the quarrel dates to October 1947. Maharajah Hari Singh of Jammu and Kashmir signed a letter of accession making his state part of the Republic of India. Over five hundred other princely rulers had already acceded, but Singh's accession produced the most far-reaching results, for Moslems formed the dominant element in this Hindu ruler's state. Almost immediately five thousand Moslem tribesmen, most of them Pathans from the Northwest Frontier, part of the new state of Pakistan, swept into Kashmir, capturing Muzaffarabad and Domela and moving to within four miles of Srinagar, Kashmir's capital.

One of the invaders, now a gun salesman in Peshawar, told me that "if there hadn't been so much to loot on the way, we would certainly have taken Srinagar."

The Indian government, for once, acted quickly. Troops were flown to Srinagar, and the invaders, laden with loot, were pushed back into what Pakistan now calls Azad (Free) Kashmir, an area constituting about 40 per cent of the total area of Kashmir. From there, with the exception of the brief Autumn War of 1965, the politicians and diplomats have taken over. They have failed lamentably to settle the issue. Indeed, intemperate speeches in both New Delhi and Rawalpindi have done much to maintain high national temperatures.

At the outset there was some doubt in the Security Council of the United Nations about the legality of Kashmir's accession to India. At this juncture the new Indian government, a staunch upholder of the principles of the United Nations except when, as in the case of Goa, these appear to conflict with Indian national interests, took the case to the Security Council. This was done on January 1, 1948; the serious fighting in Kashmir had then been over for some time, although some guerrilla activity continued. But India had the military situation firmly under control, and the moment for an appeal to the world organization appeared advantageous to India. The Kashmir issue was referred to the Security Council:

> In order to avoid any possible suggestion that India had taken advantage of the State's immediate peril for her own political advantage, the Dominion [Indian] Government made it clear

that once the soil of the state had been cleared of the invader and normal conditions were restored, the people would be free to decide their future by the recognized democratic method of plebiscite or referendum, which, in order to ensure complete impartiality, may be held under international auspices.

Time, propaganda, and national passions have distorted the Kashmir story. But in retrospect it seems clear that, from India's standpoint, the submission of the Kashmir case to the Security Council was a diplomatic error. True, a United Nations Commission investigated the situation and United Nations Observers supervised the establishment of a cease-fire line in 1947 and again in 1965. But Pakistan repeatedly has demanded, with some reason, as the Indian statement quoted above shows, the "plebiscite or referendum" promised in 1948. The Indians respond that because Pakistan has never surrendered the 40 per cent of Kashmir held as Azad Kashmir and because the people of Jammu and Kashmir have exercised their right to self-determination in three local elections since 1947, the Indian government is no longer required to fulfill the 1948 pledge.

The Indians point out that the United Nations Commission for India and Pakistan, in a resolution of August 13, 1948, accepted by both India and Pakistan, reported that "as the presence of troops in Pakistan in the territory of the State of Jammu and Kashmir constitutes a material change in the situation since it was presented by the Government of Pakistan before the Security Council, the Government of Pakistan agrees to withdraw its troops from that State." Again, this Pakistani agreement has never been implemented.

The situation smoldered for eighteen years. Then, in the late summer of 1965, it exploded. A great deal of oratory has been spilled over the question of who actually began the Autumn War. But whether the Indian or the Pakistani army fired the first shot now seems irrelevant. It was perfectly clear in August 1965 that

131

well-armed Pakistanis, variously described as infiltrators, irregulars, or commandos, were moving into Kashmir and inciting and promoting uprisings among the Moslem population against their Indian rulers. When the fighting intensified, the Moslems would call for help from their Pakistani brothers and the Pakistani army would respond by invading Kashmir. Such, at any rate, appears to have been the plan.

The fighting between the two armies exploded after Indian army forces moved into Azad Kashmir in late August to occupy positions in the Tithwal and Uri-Punch sectors. At first light on September 1, the Pakistani armored division rumbled into the Akhnur area of Jammu in an action which the Indians considered an invasion of Indian soil. The war began.

It was a short war, notable for the abandonment by both sides of the normal niceties of conduct toward diplomats of the enemy power, for the mendacity of the communiqués on each side, and for the showers of vituperation and abuse hurled by the Pakistanis upon the Indians and the Indians upon the Pakistanis. The two superpowers, the United States and the Soviet Union, finally agreed in the Security Council of the United Nations on a formula calling for a cease-fire. The Security Council's order became effective on September 23, and the war was over.

The Kashmir situation was dangerous enough within its original dimensions: a quarrel between the two largest states in southern Asia exacerbated by violent nationalist and religious passions. But today it has become infinitely more dangerous because of the intervention of a third power, Communist China, on the side of Pakistan and the military support being given India by the Soviet Union.

Chinese military pressure on India first developed in the autumn of 1962 when a series of clashes took place between Indian and Chinese troops in Ladakh and the Northeast Frontier Agency. The Indians had the worst of it. But a lesser development during the Autumn War proved more sinister. This was the presentation on September 17 by Peking of an ultimatum to India, demanding the demolition by India of fortifications allegedly built by the Indians in the Nathu-La Pass on the Tibetan side of the frontier between Tibet and Sikkim. The Indian reply was conciliatory. It agreed to the demolition of the structures, if they were found on the Tibetan side of the frontier, and offered joint inspection of the frontier where the Indians were supposed to have established fortifications. Given India's expanding military involvement in the war with Pakistan, this soft answer is understandable enough.

What is not understandable is the shock to Indian sensibilities by Chinese belligerence first in 1962 and again in 1965. From the outset Prime Minister Nehru's India had done its best to make friends with the Chinese, professing a common interest in leading Asia toward a new stature in the world. The idea of Sino-Indian amity was cherished by Mr. Nehru and his followers while, at the same time, the Chinese worked industriously to weaken India's diplomatic position in the rest of Asia. India, the apostle of nonalignment, seldom missed an opportunity to censure the United States, China's chief obstacle to hegemony in Asia, or to lecture other governments on the folly of considering the Chinese an aggressive, expansionist people. The invasion of Tibet, the fighting in 1962, and the ultimatum of 1965 have dissipated the old fanciful view of Sino-Indian relations. The Indians now know what they are up against.

The Chinese support for Pakistan in 1965 has had two consequences. The first and immediate one was to convince the United States and the Soviet Union that, whoever was responsible for the Autumn War, it must be stopped. So the two delegations to the Security Council agreed on a cease-fire order in a hurry. The specter of Chinese troops coming to the aid of the hard-pressed Pakistanis sufficed to ensure diplomatic celerity. The

Security Council resolution, in common with most resolutions of that august body, did not of course go to the heart of the matter. The central area of conflict between the two governments over Kashmir was left untouched, aside from the usual vague promises. But the fighting was ended and the United Nations indulged in the round of self-congratulation that is customary whenever the organization has managed to *appear* effective.

The second consequence was the movement by Moscow toward more diplomatic and military support for India. In the field of arms supply, this began after the 1962 confrontation, when the Soviets began to make up some of India's military deficiencies by sending helicopters and other arms and equipment to the Indians. When, during the Autumn War, the United States and Britain halted the supply of arms to both India and Pakistan, the Russians stepped up their armaments shipments to the Indians. India, in the months after the war, faced dangerous military situations on both her northern and northwestern frontiers, the one resulting from the existence of a shaken but still dangerous Pakistani army and air force, the other from the presence of fourteen Chinese divisions in Tibet.

The Russians took the initiative in arranging the meeting between Prime Minister Lal Bahadur Shastri of India and President Mohammed Ayub Khan of Pakistan at Tashkent in the Soviet Union. From this came the Declaration of Tashkent, the closest approximation to an armistice agreement possible under the circumstances of the Kashmir dispute.

Under it the two governments agreed to exert all efforts to create good relations and to settle disputes without the use of force in accordance with the Charter of the United Nations, to withdraw all armed personnel to the positions held before August 5, 1965, to avoid interference in each other's internal affairs, and to discourage hostile propaganda and promote good relations. The Declaration also provided for meetings at "all levels" to discuss matters of direct concern to both parties and the establishment of joint Indian-Pakistani groups to report to both governments.

Naturally the Russians presented this declaration as a triumph of Soviet diplomacy. Actually it was nothing of the sort because, like previous United Nations declarations, it avoided coming to grips with the basic issue: the dispute between the two governments over whether or not a plebiscite or referendum should be held in Jammu and Kashmir.

Elsewhere in Asia we have seen Communist China as a political, economic, and military threat to the independence and freedom of smaller states. This threat in 1966 and 1967 lost some of its menace because of the preoccupation of China's leaders with the Cultural Revolution. Yet it exists in all its dread potential for democratic leaders as different as President Ferdinand Marcos of the Philippines and Prime Minister Lee Kuan Yew of Singapore. Now, in India, we find a major nation, whose survival is of the maximum importance to independence and democracy in Asia, face to face with overt Chinese pressure. The focal point for this pressure is Ladakh in Kashmir. As long as the Chinese continue to occupy it and to exert pressure there, no Indian government is likely to be willing to discuss a settlement with China's friends in Pakistan.

Ladakh is of great military importance to China. Across the northeast corner of that region's Aksai Chin plateau runs the Yehch'eng–Tibet highway built by the Chinese in the late fifties. This connects Yarkand and Khotan in Sinkiang with Gartok in Tibet, and over it flow the supplies necessary to maintain the Chinese divisions in Tibet. Over it would move, in the event of war, other divisions to be employed against India. Obviously, if the road is to remain open to this kind of traffic, China must retain its grip on northeastern Ladakh. It is equally obvious that it is in China's interests to maintain unrest in Kashmir, helped by the Pakistanis, because such unrest may serve as the future basis for a War of National Liberation and the establishment of an "independent" Kashmir subservient to China. As we will see, the Pakistanis, who now boast of an intimate knowledge of China similar to that the Indians believe they enjoyed a decade ago, scoff at this. But the Pakistanis are riding the tiger.

There are other advantages to China in the present Indian-Pakistani enmity. As long as it continues, India is in no position to try and recover Ladakh from China. There is very little chance that under present conditions India and Pakistan could ever agree to a joint policy to halt Chinese infiltration into the border regions of both countries.

The military defense of the kingdoms of Sikkim and Bhutan is by treaty India's responsibility.

These two kingdoms on the roof of the world are key areas in the contest brewing along the 2,640-mile-long frontier between the two great Asian powers. From Tibet, the Chinese look westward toward Kashmir and Pakistan, southward into Nepal, Sikkim, and Bhutan, and southeastward into the Northeast Frontier Agency. Parts, and in some cases all, of these areas are claimed by the Chinese on various grounds. Sikkim and Bhutan, the Chinese say, were seized by British imperialists between 1840 and 1919. Since both nations in the past paid tribute to Tibet, and Tibet is now part of China, Peking argues that the states are Chinese. In the case of Nepal the argument is that in the late eighteenth century Nepal's rulers were tributaries to the Emperor of China, a claim about as valid as a British claim to Aquitaine in France as a result of its inclusion in the England of the Plantagenets. Nonetheless, this bit of mythological diplomacy has been refurbished by Peking and presented to the world as a serious claim.

India's position today in these frontier areas is weakened by memories of interference, especially in Nepal in the days when

Mr. Nehru was acting the role of universal aunt with gusto. Mounting Chinese influence in Nepal has forced the Indians to try and make amends for earlier interference. But in New Delhi, Indian diplomats gloomily conceded that Chinese influence in Katmandu, Nepal's capital, was more robust than India's and that they had encountered serious difficulties in impressing upon the Nepalese the gravity of China's threat to their freedom.

To overawe Sikkim and Bhutan and their Indian garrisons, the Chinese have concentrated the best troops of their Tibet garrison in the Chumbi valley, part of Tibet that the British regarded as a dagger pointed at the heart of India. From the strategic point of view the valley probably is the most dangerous spot on the whole frontier. Five passes, the Choko La, Yak La, Nathu La, Jelep La, and Dongkya La, lead from the valley into Sikkim. From Sikkim two modern highways run into India. Should China win control of Sikkim and move into these roads, she would be in a position to threaten the severance of Assam, parts of Bengal, and the Northeast Frontier Agency from the rest of India. These are high stakes.

Perhaps the most sinister diplomatic element in the situation is China's refusal to recognize Bhutan and Sikkim as protectorates of India. To worried Indian officials in New Delhi in May of 1967 this was an indication that the Chinese are preparing the diplomatic foundation for any future military moves they may contemplate after the "Cultural Revolution" has run its course.

The situation, then, along India's northern frontiers is infinitely sinister. The states there offer opportunities for Peking's favorite form of foreign interference, the fomenting of "Wars of National Liberation."

Success in such wars would shake the whole structure of Indian unity; the loss of Kashmir alone, most Indians concede, could wreck the Union. Moreover, continued military pressure in this area will impose on the already weakened Indian economy almost unbearable burdens in defense expenditure. The situation is dangerous now; it could become desperate overnight.

The primary Indian response to the northern threat has been to assign a large section of the army to guard the northern frontiers, as large a force as can be spared from the watch on Pakistan in Kashmir. The army in that area appears in much better shape, quantitatively and qualitatively, than that which failed to distinguish itself in the 1962 fighting. It is, however, committed to a system of linear defense which strikes many foreign military men in New Delhi as an invitation to trouble. Should the Chinese punch through this defense, they reason, there will be little to bar their way into India herself, because most of the best troops are assigned to linear defenses elsewhere on the frontier. The Indian Army in 1967 comprised twenty-seven divisions; China had fourteen divisions in Tibet alone.

The principal interest of the United States in both India and Pakistan, Ambassador Chester Bowles said, is to "curb the arms race" between the two countries. India's principal interest is to obtain the arms necessary to withstand Chinese aggression or, at least, to demonstrate that such aggression would be costly. In this situation New Delhi has turned increasingly toward the Soviet Union.

Russian military aid takes two forms. Soviet technicians have been installed in Indian armaments and aircraft plants to supervise the making of MIG fighters for the Indian Air Force. Meanwhile the Soviet Union has sold India over five hundred TU-54 and TU-55 tanks, large quantities of antitank and antiaircraft guns, and other military stores. The most important Soviet arms aid proposal came early in 1967 when Moscow offered to sell India at least two hundred Sukhoi 7's, at a cost of about 400 million dollars. The Sukhoi 7 is a long-range multipurpose fighter. Its acquisition by the I.A.F. would more than balance the acquisition of Mystère fighters bought by Pakistan from France.

Indian rearmament, of course, is only one aspect of defense against China. But it is a costly one. Defense spending in 1967 was running at about 3.7 per cent of India's Gross National Product or between 1.3 and 1.5 billion dollars annually. Equally important and more difficult to organize is India's internal political defense against Communist subversion. Yet a visitor finds Indian politicians and officials concentrating mainly on the military problem, as though this were 1956 and the Congress Party the unchallenged political boss of India.

Officials at the Ministry of External Affairs conceded growing Chinese influence in East Pakistan, which is adjacent to the restless Bengal where Communists are numerous and active. This influence, they said, "might" encourage separatists in West Bengal, where agitation against the central government by a coalition of left-wing parties had reached a dangerous level.

But the government's principal preoccupation was with Chinese military pressure and Chinese collusion with Pakistan over Kashmir. From the Indian standpoint the situation revolves around Pakistan's ambitions in Kashmir. Now that the Chinese are an active element in the dispute, the Indians cannot believe with any real confidence that Kashmir's future is settled forever as an integral part of the Indian Union.

Is there a way out? The only bargaining position mentioned by the Indians was a willingness to renounce the Indian claim to the 40 per cent of Kashmir, Azad Kashmir, now held by the Pakistanis, in return for the abandonment by the Pakistan government to its "claim" to Kashmir. This supposed concession by New Delhi, the Pakistanis said, misses the point of their position. They are not "claiming" Kashmir but only asking India to fulfill a twenty-year-old promise to allow the state self-determination. Pakistan, they insist, will abide by any outcome of the voting, provided it is supervised by some international authority.

Indian concentration on the Kashmir-Pakistan-China issue is an obstacle to the establishment of stronger ties between India and the states of Southeast Asia. So is the record of Indian diplomacy since ·independence, which has paid more attention to the countries of the Middle East and Africa than it has to its neighbors to the southeast. India's lack of interest in the affairs of that turbulent area and its policy of nonalignment in the contest between communism and the independent states understandably created the impression in Southeast Asia that the Indians basically were on China's side.

India offered no support to Malaysia when it was confronted by Indonesian threats. Thailand has often been bitterly criticized in India because of her membership in SEATO. Liberal Indian opinion has been highly critical of United States intervention in South Vietnam and of the assistance given the government and people of that country by other Asian states. Finally India has been incredibly cavalier in its treatment of Japan.

In 1967 there were signs that India's attitude toward these neighbors was beginning to change. Prime Minister Gandhi's freedom of action was to some extent circumscribed by the narrowness of her parliamentary majority. But all political parties, except, of course, the Communists and their allies, recognized that India's peace and prosperity depended in the future on peace and prosperity in the arc of countries running from Japan to Burma. This, at least, is a start away from noninvolvement.

India at this writing, unfortunately, has little to offer. The economy is slowly emerging from a depression. Indian military strength is so concentrated against China and Pakistan that there is little but promises to offer states in Southeast Asia after restoring its economic and political ties with the area; the power base on which she must operate is woefully weak.

Indian politics are in a state of transition, a factor that argues against the adoption of bold new policies at home or abroad.

The Congress Party that led India to independence and governed it thereafter suffers from the ills of all parties that have been in power too long. Even after the severe losses in the elections early in 1967, Congress politicians exuded an almost unbelievable complacency. They lived in the past.

The picture on the whole is not an optimistic one. Yet there are some reasons for optimism. One is that the Indian population, especially the agricultural population, is slowly, very slowly, moving into this century by turning from a subsistence agriculture to cash crops. Life in the villages, the social and political core of India, is no longer static; the farmers will expand their production as quickly as they can get the fertilizers and the implements. The agricultural population is, in the economists' jargon, becoming "production oriented" rather than "consumer oriented."

Another reason for optimism is the toughness of the people. I am not talking here about the polished Indian diplomats and officials, so free with their advice to other countries, so high-minded about affairs which they do not think affect India, but of the Indian of the villages and the city streets. Here is an almost superhuman patience and endurance that seems to say, "We, the people of India, can endure much because we have endured so much in the past, and because of this endurance we will survive and we will build."

Whatever the outcome of India's travail, the harsh imperatives of India's relations with the rest of the world remain. If India falls apart under Chinese pressure or through Communist subversion, Southeast Asia's position is hopeless. Consequently, the United States must help India survive and must induce her leaders to look east to Southeast Asia and Japan rather than to the Middle East and Africa. For quite obviously the United States cannot base its position in Southeast Asia on the countries of that area alone or on allies like South Korea, the Philippines, Australia, and New Zealand. The weight needed to ensure the establishment of a counterpoise to China can be provided only by a viable India and Japan at the two ends of the Asian arc.

To repeat, such a policy on India's part will require the abandonment of cherished aspects of Indian policy. Friendship and close ties with Southeast Asia and Japan cannot be accomplished by leadership of the Afro-Asian bloc. Preaching non-alignment cannot be reconciled with a policy of building an Asian bloc strong enough to resist Chinese pressure.

The Indians are attracted and encouraged by Soviet military help and diplomatic support. In their present desperate position vis-à-vis China, this is essential. Those Indians who advocate stronger ties with Southeast Asia believe these ties could be reconciled with the continuation of close relations with the Soviet Union. However, to take the very long view, the creation of a group of strong anti-Chinese states in South and Southeast Asia might not be in the ultimate interests of the Soviet Union. For would not the Chinese, if they found themselves blocked to the south and southeast, begin to eye the empty stretches of Soviet Central Asia?

But the ultimate question is whether India can remain a united country and continue progress toward a viable economy, changing in the progress from a traditional society to one based on science and technology. There were no satisfying answers in New Delhi.

To Indian nationalists the country's troubles are magnified by malignant outsiders. To critical foreigners the corruption of the government and the sloth of the Indian worker make progress impossible. To the villager, even today far more isolated than his counterparts in the Soviet Union or Japan, India's problems boil down to his own personal difficulties.

If there is an answer it lies within India. What India does herself, to herself, for herself is what will count. The solution does not lie in Peking or Pakistan or in Moscow or Washington.

How good are the chances of India's regeneration and survival as an independent union? In May of 1967 the best informed in New Delhi's diplomatic colony put them at no more than 60–40.

VII

Pakistan: The Lost Friend

Pakistan is an old friend who has forgotten you. Pakistan is an uncertain, brash adolescent who doesn't know how to choose his friends. Pakistan is the pattern for Asian nations of the future: independent, tough, opportunistic. Pakistan is the old Asia too deeply involved in irrelevant, unimportant quarrels to play a significant role in the making of the future.

I heard all these descriptions of the country in Karachi, Rawalpindi, Islamabad, and Peshawar. There is a smidgen of truth in each. Yet all skirt the main, the overwhelming fact. Pakistan is a country whose close neighbors include the three most populous nations on earth: Communist China, India, and the Soviet Union. Pakistan's geographical situation, and a dozen other considerations make her vitally important to peace in southern Asia.

That geographical situation, a country wedged between India, China, and Russia, is the start. Because of it, we find in Pakistan a brusque defensive independence of the West, an expanding economic and political friendship with China, and, finally and most dangerous, an almost paranoiac attitude toward India. These are dangerous—in the context of world peace—admirable, and exciting people: passionate and turbulent, God-fearing and industrious. There is no single pattern into which Pakistan can be squeezed. The Pakistanis are a greater force than the Indians, but a lesser people.

Larger, more powerful, and often irresponsible neighbors affect different countries in different ways. The Dutch and Polish people, for example, have never been cowed by neighboring giants or subdued for long by occupying powers. The Belgians and the Rumanians, more often than not, have sought the easy way out. Pakistan has followed the first pattern with every excuse for following the second. There are perhaps 700 million Chinese, more than 500 million Indians, and upwards of 200 million Russians across her frontiers. Far from being awed by these masses, Pakistan, a nation of perhaps 125 million, has adopted a belligerent nationalism.

This is a state of mind that lends itself to exaggeration. In tones of the utmost solemnity, experienced and responsible Pakistani officials told me that India, convinced that Pakistan plans to revive the Moghul Empire, has prepared plans for the conquest of their country. India, they said darkly, has never forgiven or forgotten the division of the old Indian Empire by the British. This nonsense, I should emphasize, did not come from street-corner orators but from diplomats and politicians of distinction. The attitude is all the more appalling when it is recognized that Pakistan and India, whatever their differences, face one mutual problem: the presence of Communist China.

And they share other joint problems: population control, agricultural improvement, separatist tendencies. Their relationship is like that of two rival West European states in the years before the arrival of Russia as a superpower forced such states into regional groupings.

Differences, unfortunately, outweigh these mutual problems. Karachi, my first stop in Pakistan, is a port, in essence little different from half a dozen others in Asia. But when the plane turns north, the visitor, no matter how insensitive, feels he is moving into another world, subtly different from India or Burma or Thailand. In the plains and mountains of north Pakistan, there is the breath, the smell, the sense of Central rather than South or Southeast Asia. The wind blows free across the roof of the world, and those green and rounded hills that rise beyond the new capital of Islamabad are the foothills of that great mountain mass that runs from Turkey to Vietnam. Here, land is elemental, dwarfing the people.

The people, too, are different. It is not only that they are Moslems. On first meeting they display a surly independence. Striding along country roads, bargaining in bazaars, courteous in explaining directions, enduring and uncomplaining in adversity, they recall to the visitor something out of the past.

Of course, this is what remains of Kipling's India. Not the babus and the pathetic English middle class lost in a land too big, too raw, for anything but conquest, but the soldiers and the tribesmen and the faithful servants. These are the Indians, as they were then, that the British liked. And, by an obvious coincidence, these were the Indians who liked the British—fought them, yes, but over the years established a durable bond that, despite the passage of time, is still there, awakened by the number of a battalion, a reference to a forgotten African battle.

About us, the Americans, they are not sure. There is a feeling in the air that somehow, somewhere, successive American administrations have failed to secure a steadfast, if not an easy, ally in these people.

One of the minor mysteries of American policy-making, of which there are not a few, is how successive administrations so completely, and perhaps irretrievably, lost the trust and the friendship of Pakistan. It is not enough to say that the judgment of Washington was that it was more important to stabilize and support India. Even in view of the hostility between New Delhi and Rawalpindi, it should have been possible, by adroit diplomacy, to keep Pakistan as a friend and ally.

What happened, from the Pakistani viewpoint, and it has seldom been ventilated in the United States, is this:

Pakistan became an ally of the United States in 1954, when she joined the South-East Asia Treaty Organization along with the United States, Britain, France, Thailand, the Philippines, Australia, and New Zealand. But even before that year, the government of Pakistan had every reason to believe that Washington regarded it as a staunch supporter of independence in southern Asia and as one of the countries on which a counterbalance to China could be built.

By 1959 the relationship between Pakistan and America had advanced to the signature of an Agreement of Cooperation under which the United States was required to come to Pakistan's assistance if she was attacked. This agreement upset the Indians, who consequently wrung from Washington an assurance that the agreement would not be directed against India. What the Eisenhower administration had in mind, as anyone but the hypersensitive Indians would have understood, was not India but China. Hypersensitivity is not a monopoly of New Delhi, however. The Pakistanis have since proved equally touchy about American aid to India.

Between 1954 and 1959 Pakistan joined the Baghdad Pact. This later became CENTO, Central Treaty Organization. This organization, of some propaganda but little military utility, had one serious effect. Soviet views on relationships with India and Pakistan were reviewed. Pakistan had become a member of what Moscow regarded as an aggressive western alliance. Parenthetically, the Russians didn't raise a howl about Pakistan's membership in SEATO; *that,* after all, was directed mainly against Communist China. The outcome of this diplomatic double take was that the Soviet Union in the United Nations and elsewhere began to back India over Kashmir against Pakistan.

After 1959 the American attitude toward India and Pakistan began to change to the disadvantage of the latter. The Pakistanis felt that the Americans were more solicitous of the interests of

India, the self-proclaimed neutral and outspoken critic of the United States, than they were of their ally, Pakistan. United States economic aid to India, for reasons I have outlined in the previous chapter, continued and expanded. India, on the basis of a Mutual Defense Assistance Agreement, was receiving military aid from the United States.

The Pakistanis pondered the situation. No one should try to haggle with a Peshawar merchant. But in certain aspects of international affairs, the Pakistanis are an elemental, almost simple people, unfitted perhaps for the tides and currents of international politics. Here they were, the sworn friends of the United States. And here were the Indians, who never missed a chance to tweak Uncle Sam's beard because of his global misdeeds, getting more economic aid and sizable military assistance. In Rawalpindi, it didn't add up.

The situation was difficult but not critical. It became critical after the fighting between India and China on the former's northern frontier in the autumn of 1962. India then began to receive military aid from the United States, Britain, and some members of the Commonwealth on a scale that the Pakistanis considered far greater than the situation warranted.

Why? Well, to Pakistanis the American military aid to India was tipping the military balance in southern Asia in favor of New Delhi — against Pakistan. India had sworn that the weapons would not be used against Pakistan. The Americans and British had said that if they were so used they would check Indian aggression. To the Pakistanis, with their deep-seated distrust of Indians and Indian policy, their wild but widely accepted fears of Indian invasion, the provision of weapons to India appeared to be the green light for a future Indian attack on Pakistan.

Here the reader might remember that fears and alarms that seem absurd in Washington or New York or Chicago seem perfectly feasible to tribesmen gossiping in the sun, to shopkeepers sipping tea in the cool of the evening. Such things, they say, are the currency of great events.

Of course, one man's danger is an easily explicable delusion to another. From the start the Pakistanis, politically and militarily, have discounted India's fears of China. The Indians lost 15,000 square miles of Kashmir, the Ladakh area, to the Chinese. But on November 21, 1962, the Chinese offered to negotiate their border differences with India and to withdraw from the territory they had overrun. India's government temporized.

President Mohammed Ayub Khan of Pakistan, an experienced soldier, held from the outset that the fighting was no more than a border clash. He considered the stories put about by New Delhi and bought by the credulous in the West, that China intended to invade India over the Himalayas in the dead of winter, were military nonsense. He believed then what Mao Tse-tung later told him in Peking: that the Indian military "provocations" had forced the Chinese to attack.

Pakistan, the faithful ally of the United States, felt that it was being placed in an inferior military position to India, the ardent neutral, which threatened Pakistan with the weapons it had been given to resist what Pakistan considered a nonexistent Chinese danger. Here was a situation that argued powerfully for a new relationship between Communist China and Moslem Pakistan.

Out the window went the old U.S.-Pakistan relationship. To the Kennedy and Johnson administrations the world was no longer black and white—Communist and anti-Communist—as it had been to John Foster Dulles. Instead this was a new rapidly changing world, in which loyalties shifted and yesterday's international values meant little today. Those immoral, neutralist Indians of Mr. Dulles's day had to be armed. America's old friends in Pakistan had to accept it. If they didn't, too bad. Had they forgotten how kind Vice-President Johnson had been to that Pakistani camel driver? So Washington reasoned as the game in southern Asia took on new dimensions and Peking raised the stakes.

The stoppage of American arms shipments to both Pakistan and India after the Autumn War in 1965 was the final disillusionment, compounded in 1967 by President Johnson's announcement that military aid would not be resumed to either country. The Administration did lift the embargo on the sale of spare parts for "lethal" military equipment. But this did not appease the Pakistanis.

As President Ayub Khan pointed out, this step could hardly be considered a concession by a country like Pakistan that was a long-standing ally of the United States. In April of 1967 Ayub Khan still sought a mutual agreement with India to reduce force levels.

"We would be very happy if both reduced their armaments," he said then. "It is a terrible burden for us. But the Indians are arming feverishly, and we need a deterrent force to defend ourselves."

He said that in India "the hard-liners are still in authority, and I see no signs of wisdom in this matter." Someone asked if the American action would force Pakistan to be more dependent on Communist China for arms. Ayub Khan quoted the Persian saying: "He who searches, finds."

What the American decision did, of course, was to confirm in President Ayub Khan's mind—and in Pakistan, that is the only mind that counts—the wisdom of looking to Peking for arms. This, however, is a good deal different from saying that she has allied herself with the Communists. The facts are that Pakistan has bought tanks and planes from China. Pakistan has been given Chinese diplomatic and political support over the Kashmir issue. The Chinese military presence in Tibet and the sporadic bursts of fire that echo down the long, narrow valleys of the Himalayas keep the Indian Army more concerned with China than with

Pakistan. Pakistan's leaders enjoy, if that is the word, a supposed intimacy with the leaders of the People's Republic of China.

But Ayub Khan is too old a soldier to leave one flank unguarded while he strengthens the other. The summer of 1967 found him busily building character in Moscow, where, on his second state visit, he did his best to convince his hosts that for Pakistan the old days of her militant anti-Sovietism as a member of the Central and South-East Asia Treaty Organizations were dead. And this being so, he could argue, is the Soviet Union's continual and increasing military aid to India any way to treat a friend? If Russia wants to keep the peace in southern Asia, the President's argument ran, then she must recognize that the constant flow of arms, from fighter planes to submarines, encourages India's ambitions against Pakistan. And if Premier Kosygin and his colleagues want to establish an enduring influence in the Arab world, won't a Soviet preference for secular India over the Islamic state of Pakistan cause some doubts among the Moslems of the Middle East? President Ayub Khan, as his diplomacy indicates, is no fool.

One strong point is his visceral realism, which breaks through just when the outsider is beginning to tire of the patriotic hyperbole of his sycophants. "Gentlemen," the President told a group of officers in the spring of 1967, "we must face the fact that we are of no great consequence to the great powers."

Two long-term ideas figure largely in the President's view on Sino-Pakistani relations and the risk of gradual Chinese subversion. One is that, as economic conditions improve in Pakistan, communism, a creed supposedly abhorrent to all good Moslems, will lose what appeal it now has among the Pakistani masses. The second is that China is not a military threat to Pakistan, that she wishes nothing from her save coexistence, and that she is "scrupulous"—the word was used a dozen times by senior officials in Rawalpindi—in pursuing a policy of nonintervention in Pakistan's internal affairs.

"There is not the slightest indication of subversion by the Chinese in Pakistan," a senior official of the foreign ministry insisted. "Look here, you must understand our position. We joined CENTO and SEATO when the United States and the Soviet Union were enemies. Now, as we see it, you're close to being friends with the Russians. Is it any wonder that, when things change that fast, we should try to establish good relations with China? The Americans are enemies of the Chinese now. But for how long? As long as the interests of the major powers change so fast, we, a small country, comparatively, must do the best we can through bilateral arrangements. We just can't antagonize China. Look at the frontiers! Look at the population! And we can't rely on the United States for arms. Mr. Johnson has proved that to us."

This eternal emphasis on arms is significant, if Pakistan's paranoia over Indian aggression is accepted, as it should be, as a motivating impulse in government policy-making. The situation is aggravated by the fact that Pakistan has no well-developed armaments industry that could provide the weapons. Consequently the Pakistanis must shop around. The United States and the Soviet Union, for basically similar reasons—fear of a Chinese invasion and military victory over India or the seizure of power in a disintegrating India by Chinese-oriented Communists —are sending the bulk of their aid to bolster the external and internal strength of the Indian government. Pakistan, therefore, buys abroad, a process complicated by a shortage of foreign exchange.

Pakistan has bought Mystère fighters from France. But by far the largest share of her arms imports comes from China; MIG-19's, a few MIG-21's, tanks, 90- and 105-millimeter guns. Neither the tanks nor the planes are as sophisticated as the American and

Soviet equipment reaching the Indians. But from the Pakistani standpoint, the urgent need overcomes tendencies to look the gift horse in the mouth. Pakistan lost about three hundred tanks in the Autumn War. Most of these have been replaced by imports from China. These are diesels. They make too much smoke. They are not easy to conceal in open country. The finish is bad; the instruments are primitive by modern standards. But they *are* tanks. They *are* available without visible strings. Pakistan's army of twelve divisions, two of them armored, needs them. Pakistan takes what it can get and swallows its pride—and its established military standards.

Among some senior officers the visitor senses a strong distaste for their reliance on the Chinese. After all, these men, like Ayub Khan, have their military roots in the West. To them the ideological convulsions of the Communist Chinese, the bizarre political quarrels of the Cultural Revolution, are repulsive as the bickering of Liberals, Laborites, and Tories were to the professional British officers who were, it should be remembered, their respected and admired guides and teachers. Indeed, the Ayub Khan regime's strongest emotional basis is a thoroughgoing dislike and distrust of any political creed, and ideology. They are, they like to say, simple soldiers. They may be, at that.

Simple enough, I fear, not to see the effect of their present relationship with China upon the balance of power in South Asia, a balance that affects Manila and Singapore quite as much as Sikkim and Nepal. What Pakistan's policy has led to, for the best motives in Pakistani eyes, is an entree for Communist Chinese power politics into a critical area of the continent.

How much Chinese influence is there? Among the rulers, pre-eminently the President and the army, almost none. Among the civil servants who execute the orders of President Ayub Khan's government, very little. The Pakistani civil service, in common with that of India, has inherited from its forebear, the old British Indian Civil Service, an austere distaste for politics as well as a high professional competence.

Yet it is impossible to be in Pakistan for long without noting among intellectuals and in the newspapers an anti-Americanism that goes beyond the natural resentment over the interruption of arms supplies or even mourning for the lost intimacy of the Dulles years.

The careful visitor notes the uses of phrases more customary in Chinese Communist propaganda statements than in a supposedly free press. Editorials on world issues seem to owe more to the persuasion of outside propaganda than they do to objective inquiry and explanation or even to fidelity to Pakistan's interest. Through the field of mass communications and through the views of the academic and journalistic elite, there runs a thread of irrationality, frequently expressed in a tendency to take an outrageously unsubstantiated view of international affairs and then to justify this view with arguments that, although satisfyingly orotund to the debater, have, in fact, no real meaning in terms of what the world is like.

The twentieth century, regrettably, has encountered this phenomenon elsewhere. It is the product of times in which proud men, ancient races, find themselves, through no fault of their own, insecure in a world they never made. Only a very old, intrinsically self-confident nation has the inner resources that enable it to accommodate the rapid changes of the era without a loss of national nerve.

One source, not the only one but certainly the most important, of Pakistan's present psychological travail is the enmity with India. Here we encounter a difference in national involvement. In India, the source of the quarrel is Kashmir. There may indeed be Indians, as the Pakistanis charge, who spend their nights plotting the overthrow of Ayub Khan and the future incorporation of his country into India. There may be, but I doubt it. The

Indians have too many other things—700 million Chinese, or is it only 650 million?—to think about, not to mention population, harvest failures, industrial development. The starting point and, to most Indians, the end of the dispute is Kashmir.

The Pakistani approach is wider, deeper. There, enmity for the Indians extends beyond the immediate issue to general distrust and hatred. The reasons? First, religious; the Moslem hatred for the Hindu is an essential part of the national attitude toward India. Pakistanis become restless when it is mentioned that the President of India is a Moslem and that there were no reported attacks on the Moslem communities—numbering about 30 million souls—in India during the Autumn War. The impression remains that the "holy war" attitude, the transfer of differences from the political to the religious sector, feeds enmity in Pakistan more than in India.

In continuing crises, such as that aroused by Kashmir, the friendly foreigner is likely to point out that some situations must be lived with, that, because they are not susceptible to early or easy settlement, governments and peoples must accept them as part of the international scene.

This sort of argument never gets off the ground in Pakistan, although some Indians accept it. It is quite evident that, in the highly charged emotional atmosphere of the country, Pakistan's government could no more renounce an active claim to Kashmir than it could renounce Islam. It is a waste of time to tell Pakistanis that the Americans and Russians have learned to live with a divided Berlin and that Pakistan must learn to live with a divided Kashmir. They answer that, although the ideological differences between Americans and Russians may be deep, they are by no means as deep as the religious and racial feud that permeates the Kashmir dispute. This Pakistani attitude should not be the subject for censure or praise. It should be understood as the way things happen to be.

The Pakistanis won't live with, won't accept, India's occupation of Jammu and Kashmir. They reject India's hints at a possible bargain by which New Delhi would meet Pakistani willingness to abandon its claim to the state by renouncing its claim to the 40 per cent of Kashmir held by the Pakistanis as Azad Kashmir. The Pakistanis insist that India has missed the point. They are not, they contend, trying to claim Kashmir as part of Pakistan. They are only asking India to fulfill an old promise to allow self-determination in Kashmir. Pakistan, they assert, will abide by the outcome of a plebiscite in Kashmir, providing it is held under international supervision.

The existence of a dispute of this magnitude in which the educated classes of a country are deeply involved creates a situation that calls for firm government, even under the most favorable conditions. But Pakistan does not enjoy favorable conditions. Her economy, like those of most developing nations, is subject to sudden starts and stops. Priorities are a matter of constant debate. Her agriculture, like India's, remains at the mercy of the weather.

Fortunately, Pakistan has a leader of extraordinary qualities. President Mohammed Ayub Khan was described by an objective foreign diplomat as "a giant among his contemporaries." He is not a giant who is always right in his judgments. This is not a leader of deep intellect or wide experience. But this is a man of character and force whose personality touches the average Pakistani; there he walks with his strong, erect stride, his bristling mustachios, his open, proud countenance; this is the happy warrior that every humble Pakistani would wish to be.

No one can listen to Ayub Khan speak or read his political autobiography, *Friends, Not Masters,* without being impressed by his personality. Indeed, his impact has been so great upon his country and upon the Asian world that the impression has developed abroad that he is an unchallenged and unchallengeable master of Pakistan.

Certainly, in the widest sense of the term, he is a dictator. Pakistan is governed by Ayub Khan. But, like certain other dictators, notably Franco, he is usually responsive to the army which made him and could, presumably, break him.

Because the loyalty of the army, and especially of the senior officers, is the basis of his authority, the President must be and is especially attentive to what the army believes and wants. The army believes, to a degree extraordinary even in this jumpy country, that it faces in the near future an attack by India. The army wants, in consequence, all the arms that Ayub Khan can obtain for it. Here is a heavy burden on a ruler.

To take the situation one step further: what would happen to Ayub Khan and his army if the quarrel with India suddenly were to be composed? This continual crisis made Ayub Khan. Would its removal break him?

The President's reputation as a soldier, his fairness, his identity with the innermost aspirations of a people that considers itself a warrior race are great political advantages. Yet criticism exists, although there was no important political opposition in 1967. Criticism centers, among the bourgeoisie, whose position as *the* important political class has been lost to the army under Ayub Khan, on the corruption that is supposed to infect the presidential "court." But the critics—in my experience, at any rate—are careful to say that the President himself is not corrupt. The charge is leveled at his relatives and friends. Ayub Khan is pictured as a sort of Asian Warren Harding, unaware of the corruption committed in his name.

The second, and perhaps the more immediately important criticism, is that Ayub Khan, in common with other leaders suddenly elevated to supreme power, finds it difficult to delegate authority. This may be due in part to the military man's ingrained suspicion of the motives, if not the efficiency, of civilian subordinates, including politicians. More, perhaps, can be attributed to the President's stubborn but not unattractive belief that he, and he alone, sees what must be done for this sprawling, divided country and that only he can generate the enthusiasm and the energy necessary to ensure the achievement of his soaring aspirations for Pakistan.

Ayub Khan suffers from his friends. In the summer of 1967 a little green book entitled *The Sayings of President Mohammed Ayub Khan* was circulated in East Pakistan by the region's governor, Abdul Monem Khan, who claimed he had the President's approval. This might well be so. Ayub Khan does so much, too much, that his approval might have been given without due thought to the parallel with the little red book incorporating the sayings of Chairman Mao Tse-tung that has been hawked over Asia by the Chinese Communists.

The President's sayings, however, have the saving virtue of horse sense in a country, indeed a continent, where the politician too often suffers from oratorical autointoxication.

"We must get out of the rut of shouting slogans and vociferous acclamations," is one saying of the President's that might be pondered and followed by his supporters. Another is, "There is only one miracle that can change the destiny of our nation, and that miracle is hard work." And, most appositely, "If nothing is done to check the rate [of population growth], I shudder to think what will happen after a few decades. My only consolation is that I shall not be there to face that situation."

There is, of course, a personality cult centered on Ayub Khan, as the publication of this booklet shows. This is bound to happen to any Asian ruler. That it has gone no further than its present modest boundaries is striking evidence of the hardheadedness of the President and his training. After all, he was raised as an officer in the British service, and officers of that service shun unprofessional conduct.

In his present situation the President can dismiss the opposition as negligible. Its leaders are aging politicians squabbling publicly over the importance of the half dozen minor parties they head. The only young, vigorous leader on the other side is Zulfikar Ali Bhutto, once Ayub Khan's Minister for External Affairs. Bhutto, rich, volatile, mercurially intelligent, a practiced, exciting orator, has a strong appeal to youth, especially the young of the universities who, in Pakistan as elsewhere in Asia, admire the radical approach of the iconoclast in politics.

Bhutto's strongest card in 1967 was his view that the country was run not by the people but by the civil service and the army and that, despite boasts of Pakistani democracy by the government, the population had little or nothing to do with major decisions of policy.

This view appeals not only to youth but to the intellectuals, those of them who have not already gone over to the government's side, as well. They feel very sorry for themselves, these people, sorry enough to promote ventures toward political alliances with the out-of-favor merchants, landowners, and bankers they once reviled.

A more serious and perhaps a more lasting challenge to the complacency of the ruler than anything offered by active politicians comes from the courts. An independent judiciary frequently disputes the government's actions as unconstitutional. Such challenges do not make headlines. The mass of the population is unaffected. But they do serve to remind the President that he is not above the law. And Ayub Khan, to repeat, is a man deeply influenced by his early environment, the British Raj, where order and discipline reigned and the law was above men.

There is no immediate, discernible threat to Ayub Khan's

continued rule. But it is easy enough to see conditions in Pakistan which, if perpetuated, could be the basis of a serious opposition. The national income per citizen is low. Wide differences exist between the standard of living of the masses and the wealthy minority. These are circumstances that could develop, in Pakistan as they have elsewhere in Asia, to the advantage of communism.

"The Communists wouldn't let the Pak masses call it communism, of course," a jovial Englishman said. "Too smart for that, those lads. Everyone knows, don't they, that communism and Islam don't mix. Certainly. So what will the Coms do? Simple enough. Get a few Moslem dignitaries to endorse a blend of Mohammedism and communism, call it any damn thing you like, and they're off and running. Don't you ever believe that the Coms have given up on the Moslems, here and anywhere else, because of the religious factor. Given sufficiently bad conditions, which they may have here in five or ten years, and communism, called, perhaps, the Moslem Revival Party, will be the hottest political force in the country."

Ayub Khan faces one other rather personal danger. He has been the biggest and, as everyone testified, the ablest man in his country for a decade. In fact, he is beginning to attract among Pakistanis the sort of emotional following that supported Prime Minister Nehru in the last years of his premiership. His identification with the country is complete. And the country is moving into that period—usually brief, but fine, heady stuff while it lasts—when it believes that it need not bother its head about problems as long as the President is there.

The obvious danger is that with the passage of time the President will become increasingly certain of his own infallibility and that the masses will sustain his interpretation of his role. When death comes, Pakistan will have lost not simply a President but a way of political life.

More than any ruler I encountered in Asia, Ayub Khan is

totally representative of his country. Prince Souvanna Phouma understands the Laotians, but his royal birth stands between him and intimacy. Madam Gandhi is a nice, intelligent woman who feels deeply for the Indian people. But this bluff, burly President of Pakistan *is* Pakistan. He suits the country. And what a country it is.

Asia is old. Elsewhere in Asia there is an almost suffocating sense of the past: of millions upon millions who passed this way before, of ruined civilizations built on ruined civilizations built on ruined civilizations. The ruins, the memorials, even so overpoweringly beautiful a structure as the Taj Mahal, seem to say, "This is the way it was; it will never be much better or much worse."

But Pakistan has a different atmosphere. The age is here, too. But the high, clean air and the mountains together proclaim an exciting future. Alexander passed this way, they say, but who knows what new conquerors may come tomorrow, what tremendous disturbances this constantly renewing land may see, what prizes its sons may win?

The distinctive flavor of the land envelops you as you leave the Rawalpindi-Islamabad government complex and drive westward toward Peshawar. Attock Fort, huge, rambling over the hills, looks down on the blue, swift Indus. Across the river the mountains seem to be toppling of their own weight on the plains.

At the bridge across the gorge of the river, the sentry is polite, using carefully his few words of English. Fish in the river? A few, not many at this time of year. Some game in the hills? Many, many—he makes a compulsive gesture with his hands to indicate the numbers—many more than when the English were here. You look at him closely. He has the lithe build, the springy step of a young man. But the face is grave and experienced; he remembers when the English were here.

The road runs now toward the Peshawar plain. The May sun

is hot but not unpleasant. This was one of the great military areas of British India, and the Pakistan Army has taken it over for its own: tank schools, drivers' schools, artillery schools, small arms, and engineers—a sergeant in the street still uses the old British word "sappers"—ordinance and signalers. Finally Peshawar, Kitchener Road and Roberts Lane, and an officer on a bay gelding riding in the sun with polo stick jauntily over his shoulder.

The bazaar at Peshawar, like the *souk* in Marrakesh, has a continental rather than a local flavor. Here the peoples of a continent mingle. Long-limbed Pathans, Pakistan Punjabis thick of chest and leg, Afghans from across the border, thin-faced, intellectual-looking men from Azad Kashmir, a few broad-faced Mongol types from the back of the mountains.

Life, not the scurrying, anxious life of Hong Kong or the resigned, wheedling life of Agra or old Delhi, hits you in the face. These are a noisy, brawling people in whom an innate courtesy for the foreigner forever quarrels with a highly developed instinct for haggling. The bazaar is alive with animals, camels, dogs, every sort of bird in the Street of Partridge Lovers. ("The municipality calls it something else," a shopkeeper said. "We go by the old names.")

There you can buy, if you have the time to bargain and the money, beautifully balanced copies of Mannlicher carbines, Lee-Enfield rifles, or Luger pistols. The stalls are rich with fruit and vegetables. The air is heavy with their scent and with other less attractive smells.

But, as they always have, the mountains call. Peshawar's plain is almost entirely surrounded by mountains, and through the roughest, if not the highest, runs the Khyber Pass.

There is one disappointment. At the entrance a sign asks the driver to go slowly, explaining, "We Love Our Children," an admonition not out of place in Elmira, New York, or Hutchinson, Kansas. But not far away is the great bulk of Fort Jamrud looking, as it frowns back at Peshawar, like some stone battleship in a sea of rock.

Civilization has made its inroads. Afridi chiefs send their daughters to Peshawar University and their sons to the Pakistan Academy for Rural Development. The government builds rural dispensaries and schools in the hill villages on each side of the pass. But civilization has not won yet. As the car begins to climb the marvelous, winding road the British built to the Afghan frontier, the present drops away. In the thin air the breeze hums through the telegraph wires; it is the only sound. On the hilltops the village forts scowl across the narrow valleys. It is lonely, desolate, and every inch of the ground you tread has known its share of blood.

When I stopped for water for the engine, a tribesman suddenly materialized out of the boulder-strewn hillside. Take a good look at him, for he and his kind are dying, killed not by bullets but by the Ford and the corner drugstore and what the West calls civilization.

He is tall, an inch or so over six feet, very lean, with broad, sloping shoulders. He wears leather sandals, long white baggy pantaloons, a dirty white shirt with the tails hanging out, and a loose turban. Over his shoulder is a copy of a British Lee-Enfield .303 rifle made at one of the tribal gun factories at Kohat to the south. The stock of the rifle shines with polishing; around the muzzle bright green and silver tinsel has been wound. The rifle is the most important article of his dress; he would feel as helpless and undressed without it as an English clerk without his umbrella.

The face was long-jawed, with a fringe of beard; bright gray eyes, a nose like a hawk's. A little English came from the wide, firm mouth. Did the sahib need any water? Was he on his way to Kabul? No, the sahib intended to go to Landi Kotal, the fort at the Pakistan side of the frontier, where both his brother-in-law and his father-in-law had served.

Ah, the "Beritish Armee, yes." Those were good days, apparently. They fought the British and then, when the British were unsporting enough to bring up planes and artillery, the tribes would hand in a few old rifles as a gesture of peace and retire to the villages to spend the long winter nights planning the next campaign.

The difference, I learned later, is that nowadays when the Pathans pick up a Pakistani official or merchant for ransom—sometimes sending a finger along with the ransom note to stress the need for haste—the Pakistanis pay up. In the old days the British sent troops, and a brisk little war flickered over the mountains and through the passes which the Pathans found entertaining until the cost became too high.

The blood feuds, which the British never interfered with, unless they hampered government business, still crackle away in the hill villages of these mountains, the Sulaiman Range. Violence is always just below the surface. Recently, they told me, a village landowner, starting for Peshawar with eggs for market, was taunted by a twenty-year-old youth. He was not a landowner, the youth gibed, just an egg peddler. The landowner shot him dead.

They are an old, free people and they nourish a haughty disdain for the Pakistanis who now, in a manner of speaking, "govern" them. Not long ago a tribesman walked into the American Consulate at Peshawar; he must have traveled a matter of twenty-five miles on foot to get there. He wanted to know if these were the people who had financed the school in his village.

They were? Well, the school was a success. He would like the Americans to come and see what had been done with their money. The consulate offered to send a man along with the local Pakistani district officer with whom the Americans worked. The tribesman said no. He did not like Pakistanis, especially that Pakistani. But if the Americans insisted, all right. The Pakistani would be allowed to come, but only this once.

Violence lives side by side with a strong strain of poetic feeling. In the evening men sit around reciting epics extolling the feats of tribal leaders. Each day the Peshawar newspapers print a full page of poetry contributed by Pathan bards. Until now the Pathans have preserved a sense of color, a rhythm of life, a joyous adventurousness.

They are an old people with a diabolical vitality. Through the Khyber Pass have marched the armies of Darius, Alexander the Great, Genghis Khan, Tamerlane, and Baber, the Great Moghul. The Pathans themselves may be the residue of some earlier Aryan invasion, left behind to scratch a living from the harsh mountains.

The Pathans fought all the *Ferrangi* (foreigners), from Alexander's spearmen to the kilted soldiers of Victoria, whose pipes awoke the echoes in the valleys with "Hey, Johnny Cope" and "The Desperate Battle." These wars are over now. And many a good man gone. And the conditions that made them are vanishing, too. But remember, when civil servants put out their propaganda about how many young Afridis have gone to school or when some desiccated official of the United Nations rejoices in the spread of civilization up the Khyber, remember that something wild and bold and free is dying up there in the passes.

But obviously these people would have little in common with the Pakistan that is developing now. Here is a country, grotesquely divided, hurrying as rapidly as it can, more rapidly in my opinion than India, into the twentieth century.

The most impressive factors were the success of the government's efforts to bind East Pakistan and West Pakistan into one state, assisted by air transport, and the sustained economic progress. Judgments are relative, of course. East Pakistan has its dissidents, its complaints that its exports finance the entire country while West Pakistan gobbles up the foreign aid. Agriculture and industry progress by fits and starts. But they do progress. And there was a willingness, unusual in a Moslem country and too often lacking among Indians, to try the new, to investigate and adopt the pragmatic approach.

The economy has demonstrated a remarkable resiliency. Neither the Autumn War nor the reduction in foreign aid halted its progress in 1966 and 1967, years that the future may see as vital to Pakistan's economic growth. The Gross National Product rose in the fiscal year 1965–66 by 5.2 per cent compared with 4.3 per cent in 1964–65. This in a year that saw the Autumn War.

Of course, the economy did not escape unscathed. Private investment fell in 1966 and 1967. Efforts to maintain the planned rate of growth encountered an adverse movement in terms of trade, which meant Pakistan was buying more than she could pay for, and the continued rise in population increased the demand for food. Here Pakistan was caught in the same situation as India; more precious funds had to be allocated for fertilizers, insecticides, and farm machinery, for irrigation projects and land reclamation schemes. The deadly contest between the yields of field and marriage bed laid its heavy hand on the government's hopes. President Ayub Khan expected a shortage of food grain of 2.5 million tons in 1966–67 and an estimated expenditure of a billion rupees, close to $500 million dollars, on food imports. Meanwhile prices continued to rise.

These are circumstances in which most Asian countries outside the Communist orbit tend to turn to the United States for help. But although there has been help aplenty in the past, and may be more in the future, Pakistan's suitability as a recipient of American aid has been drastically reduced by her flirtation with Peking. The flow of United States aid was cut in 1965–66, the first year of Pakistan's third Five-Year Plan, as a consequence of Rawalpindi's movement toward friendship, but not alliance, with Communist China. Naturally, the Pakistanis have since tried to seek aid from other quarters and to diversify their foreign trade.

Here, again, we see the remarkable resilience of the Pakistanis at work. Despite the war with India and despite pressures on the currency, Pakistan's foreign trade continued to expand. Production of exports rose, and the balance-of-trade position, which had been unfavorable for a number of years, showed definite signs of improvement.

Markets were the problem. Pakistan found them in barter arrangements with the Soviet Union, Poland, Hungary, Yugoslavia, Bulgaria, and Communist China. Special arrangements were made with Indonesia, Turkey, and Iran. The result was that Pakistan's exports to these countries doubled in 1965-66, and they were sure in Rawalpindi that the prospects for 1966-67 would be even better.

In this process we can see, certainly we *should* see, the gradual movement of a country by early tradition and initial alliances strongly favorable to the West into an intimate economic relationship with the Communist bloc. The United States is losing a friend, which is not unusual these days; it may also be in the process of losing a valuable trading partner for the future.

Perhaps it is the beguiling attraction of a single-minded purpose, always to be found in an authoritarian state in comparison with a democracy, and often misleading, that creates in the visitor's mind the impression that the Pakistanis know where they are going and how they are going to get there and the Indians do not.

Pakistan boasts the infrastructure of competitive industry: iron and steel mills, factories for machine tools and automotive products, plants for petrochemicals. But Pakistan, at the same

167

time, has managed to raise the production of primary products processed in the country. Jute products, for example, have risen sharply in output. Cotton yarn and cotton cloth, however, have shown a slight decline in production. Yet the over-all outlook is favorable. A steel mill, that hallmark of progress in a developing country, is in production at Chittagong, and its capacity is to be extended.

Granted the chauvinism that influences Pakistani government statements and, it is feared, government statistics, the outlook for an expanding industry is favorable. Of course, in Pakistan, as in every country from the Philippines westward, the traveler sooner or later finds himself face to face with the basic social-economic issue: population vs. food. Economic growth was perhaps 20 per cent between 1960 and 1965. But this had no real meaning to the average citizen because population growth in the same period almost nullified the effect of the rise in Gross National Product on the majority of the people. Here again we must assimilate those foreboding statistics that spell out the harsh future for an Asian country.

The population of what is now Pakistan doubled between 1901 and 1961. The rate of population growth between 1961 and 1971 is expected to vary between 2.7 per cent and 3.2 per cent. Even if the family planning program, now strongly supported by the government, makes a noticeable impact on the increase in population, Pakistan probably will still have to accommodate an annual population increase of 2.5 per cent. Any check to the expansion of the Gross National Product, as provided in the third Five-Year Plan, will, in conjunction with population growth, end the government's hopes for rapid development of education, health, and social welfare.

In those circumstances Pakistan will be able either to feed the people or give them more schools and hospitals. The government won't be able to do both. Yet present projections for expenditure in these fields are higher than ever before. In education they reflect an awareness, often absent in Asia, of the need to tailor education to meet the needs of a developing economy rather than the requirements of an overloaded bureaucracy.

Thus Pakistan's basic goals in developing education are first to provide a system that will ease the transition from an agrarian economy into an era of science and technology, next to establish conditions that will give young people an opportunity to develop individual capacities and character, and finally to raise the general quality of education.

All very laudable. But all, again, dependent on self-sufficiency in food and a lowering of the population rate in the future. Again the visitor develops a split personality. Hours of listening to young, enthusiastic officials is apt to convince him that Pakistan can do all it plans: self-sufficiency in food by 1970, full employment and accommodations for all children of school-going age by 1970. Then, wandering around the countryside or talking to people in forgotten villages, the terrible magnitude of the task overwhelms him and the efforts of those young, enthusiastic officials seem no more meaningful than a furrow drawn in sand.

Family planning, in the government's view, should become a mass movement reaching from the village midwife to the city clinic. President Ayub Khan from the start has been a powerful advocate of the program and has recognized that the key to success lies in the family planning official who directs the program in twenty-five or thirty villages, providing loops, the pill, guidance, and medical advice. By mid-1967, there were three million loops in use in Pakistan. Two factories were making the pills, more were being imported, a nationwide propaganda campaign emphasized the social and economic benefits of limiting a family to two children. This way, the billboards said, leads to happiness.

The reader will see in this program the same drives, the same goals that animate the Indians who share the subcontinent. The difference is that the Pakistani agriculture is in far better shape to cope with the present high birth rate than is India's.

Pakistan, as we have seen, still must import wheat, coarse grains, and rice. But given favorable weather, the outlook is hopeful for 1967 and 1968. The introduction of the miracle rice, IR-8, in East Pakistan has increased yields there even in areas where three crops a year are customary. In the wheat-growing areas of West Pakistan the introduction of new strains of wheat has resulted in a comparable increase in yield. In both regions the government emphasizes the importance of increasing the production of existing acreage through the introduction of new strains and the wider use of fertilizers, pesticides, and irrigation.

"We will be self-sufficient in wheat by nineteen seventy with a gross crop of seventy million tons in West Pakistan," the bright young men tell you in Rawalpindi, "and self-sufficient in rice in the same year with a crop of thirteen million tons from both regions."

This sort of pie in the sky is the lingua franca of Asian official-dom. But two developments in Pakistan provide some basis for this optimism. On the farms I visited, unaccompanied by government tub thumpers, there was an avid eagerness to use new methods, new fertilizers. As has happened elsewhere in Asia, and as still happens in the boondocks of the Philippines, fertilizers had to be forced on the farmers at the outset. Now, if none are available through the regular channels, groups of farmers will pool their resources to buy fertilizers on the black market. Similarly, the East Pakistan rice farmers who originally resisted the introduction of IR-8 have now learned its effect on yields.

"I was a fool," a young farmer in East Pakistan said. "I used only half the seed they gave me. I know better now. Is it, in truth, an American thing?"

His question reflected a condition very widespread in Pakistan. The farmers are benefiting from new strains of rice and wheat introduced by American aid programs, federal and private, but in so chauvinistic a country the origin of these improvements often is obscured by nationalistic officials. Again, we must consider that these officials, reading the obedient press, are given the impression day after day that the United States is hostile to Pakistan and its people. Why, then, should they dwell upon the American bounty?

The second factor working for continued expansion of Pakistani agricultural production is the steady progress toward land reform. It would be inaccurate to say that this has been accomplished completely. But the last ten years have seen a steady elimination of the tenant-farmer class, the sharecroppers who had no incentive. Land has been returned to the state and then redistributed. A class of yeoman farmer is developing with its eye on cash crops and steady improvement of the land. Individual holdings once scattered over a wide area have been consolidated into large farms. The farmers' private investments in tube wells, fertilizers, machinery, and pesticides are increasing.

Is the picture too glowing? Perhaps; Pakistan's problems are as great, if not as large in size, as those that face India. The difference, to repeat, seemed to be in the more enthusiastic response of the Pakistani farmer to new methods and to the vitality of the government's program, from planning offices in Rawalpindi down to agricultural agents on the farms.

The question that must concern all Americans interested in Asia and our country's future there is where Pakistan goes from here. We know the political and economic outlines of the problem.

Here is a large country, once closely tied to the United States, that has moved out of the western orbit into increasing coopera- tion with Communist China. Here is a country with a grievance, Kashmir, that could cause a conflagration in the subcontinent compared with which all the fighting in South Vietnam, Laos, and Thailand would seem like small boys bickering in the streets. Pakistan has grave economic, social, and political problems, none of which are in sight of solution.

The United States has for the moment reduced its political involvement in Pakistan's future. One hears in Rawalpindi a complaint monotonously repeated in other Asian and most Euro- pean capitals: the United States, involved in the Vietnamese war, has no time for us or our problems. And, the more presci- ent add, when the United States does recognize the importance of the country and its problems, it will be too late.

Of course, in international as in domestic politics, it is foolish to say that any policy is final. Recent history, especially in Europe, is too full of examples of enemies' hands clasped in friendship, of policies abandoned and then revived. But granted the independent, sensitive nature of the Pakistanis, we have gone a long way down the road to ensuring their hostility to American policy. It is argued that, in exchange, we have won the friendship of India and that this balances any loss of influ- ence in Pakistan. And what has that friendship been worth? When and where has India publicly supported American policy: in the Middle East, in Southeast Asia?

Unfortunately the future course of Pakistan seems to depend more on how the Communist Chinese play their cards there than on anything the United States may belatedly do to restore con- fidence in our policies. The Chinese position in Pakistan could be exploited to the detriment of peace in the subcontinent and, naturally, to American influence there. Such exploitation has not been pushed to the limit by the Chinese, apparently because of the government's preoccupation with the Cultural Revolution. This does not mean that it *can* not or *will* not be exploited to the full in the future. The Chinese would be very stupid indeed if they did not take advantage of the position that their arms and their diplomatic and political support gives them over the United States or any combination of western nations in Pakistan.

American statesmanship faces a challenge in Pakistan unparalleled in its importance elsewhere in independent Asia. For all the surliness of the Pakistani officials, for all the resentment over the arms embargo, there remains a residual element of esteem and friendship. This could be used to America's advantage once the Pakistanis are convinced that we are not taking sides with India against them, that we do not wish to penalize them because, in a desperate hour, they turned north to Peking for help, that we are as interested in the success of their battle to develop their country as we are in India's or Turkey's.

The challenge is worth meeting. The importance of the India-Pakistan-Kashmir situation requires no emphasis. If China becomes, as she is on the way to becoming, Pakistan's lone great friend in the world, then the chances of Pakistan's being led into a new war with India over Kashmir increase. Such a war will certainly wreck the subcontinent. The eventual winner will be neither India nor Pakistan, but Communist China. The first step in averting it is the restoration of United States influence in Pakistan.

This will not be easy. Pakistan may want, as President Ayub Khan says, to be friends with everyone. But in her present position she can afford to be friends only with those countries whose attitude toward her is recognized as friendly in Rawalpindi because of deeds, not words.

One other point is worth emphasizing. The Six Days' War in the Middle East in June 1967 sounded alarm bells in every Islamic country, and the alarm was sounded against the United

States as a result of the Administration's support for Israel. Pakistan is a big, relatively powerful Islamic state. It is all too clear that in the coming years America will need big, powerful friends among such states. Pakistan could be such a friend.

Nothing I saw or heard in Pakistan gave the impression that the United States is now willing to make the effort—or, indeed, if it wished to make this effort, that the Administration had the sophistication or the finesse to make it successfully.

Pakistan, indeed, is a friend who has forgotten you. The tragedy is that in the present circumstances no one thinks it worth the effort to restore an old friendship. So Pakistan, tough, independent, hurt, may go blundering into the arms of China and loose an explosion that will set Asia afire.

VIII

The Extremes of Fortune: Iran, Afghanistan, the Philippines, Indonesia

The Asia we have seen thus far is one where war and threats of war and thoughts of war dominate. But there also are Asian countries where peace and progress advance, where a rough cooperation has been worked out among the interested great powers. On the other hand there are states where acute economic difficulties, and the corruption, lawlessness, and political immorality they produce, have created situations so grave that the peoples and governments seem sliding, literally before our eyes, into chaos.

To move from South and Southeast Asia into Iran is like leaving the jungle for a well-ordered zoo. Here the problems that challenge and often overwhelm other Asian governments have been met and to a large extent controlled, if not entirely conquered. In Teheran the visitor senses a feeling unusual in Asia: that of achievement. With reason, too. The Iranian economy is growing at the rate of about 12 per cent annually, and the per capita income has just about doubled in the last ten years.

Oil, of course, is a large part of the answer. But not the whole answer. Other countries have oil in plenty; none has used oil field earnings as wisely as Iran. Today oil is the basis of an expanding economy, not the entire economy. Oil revenues have been invested to expand cotton acreage, to build dams to irrigate rice fields, to promote land reform and education, to pull the huge country together with highways, railroads, and airlines.

In the process Iran has been able gradually to resume control of its destiny. "Iranians run Iran," a young government official boasted at a dinner party, and he was right. Teheran is remarkably free of the foreign technicians, advisers, and administrators encountered in other Asian capitals. Iran no longer depends on them or on outside aid for economic progress. On the contrary, foreign companies are eager to invest in Iran; foreign investment is approaching one and a half billion dollars.

The driving force in this great national effort is Mohammed Reza Pahlavi, the Shah. He and his country are worth a book. But for this short account two outstanding feats of the Shah and his people must be recorded.

He has transformed, admittedly with a great deal of American aid and with the sure basis of the oil revenues, a backward, stagnant country into one of the most progressive and vital in Asia. And, in the process, he has been able to steer a safe and honorable course through the tumultuous politics of southern Asia and the Middle East. Iran is a land bridge between these two critical areas. Her southeastern frontier touches Pakistan. To the north lies the Soviet Union. The western border marches with the borders of Turkey and Iraq.

Iran is a Moslem but not an Arab state. The Shah has moved surefootedly through recurrent crises in the Middle East. He and his government are on good terms with Iraq, Turkey, Kuwait, and other moderate elements in that strife-ridden area, but the Shah considers President Gamal Abdel Nasser of the United Arab Republic a feckless trouble-maker whose policies could ruin the Middle East.

By training and by habit of thought the Shah is a Westerner. But his careful diplomacy has improved relations with the Soviet Union. These became strained in the immediate postwar years when Russia, watching the British withdrawal from India, saw Iran as a field for Soviet political and economic expansion. The support of the Americans and the British in those years and the development, albeit a bit belated, of firmness by the Shah warned off the Russians. Since then the Soviet bloc has invested heavily in Iran, building a steel mill and other heavy industrial installations in return for oil and natural gas.

As a continental Asian country that is in a fair way to mastering its internal problems, Iran is not unique. Malaysia and Thailand, as we have seen, have both registered considerable economic progress despite the lowering presence of Communist China on their northern frontiers. In Afghanistan, the United States and the Soviet Union in unacknowledged cooperation are doing their utmost to raise a backward Asian state from poverty to prosperity.

The American and Soviet officials who administer their countries' respective aid programs in Afghanistan cannot be said to cooperate openly. They do confer and exchange ideas at the Ministry of Planning which directs Afghanistan's economic modernization.

"Anything can happen here," Afghans are happy to tell the visitor. As proof, they cite the fact that in the spring of 1967 the Soviet aid group told the Afghan government to take the advice of the United States and expand private enterprise in the country; a development comparable to President Johnson's telling the Brazilians to try a little communism to cure their economic ills.

Highways built by the two aid groups "happen" to meet at nodal points, experts confer on mutual problems, and information about local conditions in distant areas is exchanged.

The Soviet Union, not the United States, is the major donor of aid for Afghanistan. Since the middle fifties, this aid has probably totaled around 600 million dollars, most of it in loans. Much of this has gone to equip the Afghan Army and Air Force. But the Soviets also built a highway to Kabul from the Russian frontier and the Naghlu hydroelectric plant. A huge natural gas field at Shibarghan on Afghanistan's northern plain is being

177

developed by Russian engineers. From 1971 some of the gas from this field will be piped to the Soviet Union to help pay for past loans.

American aid, largely in the form of grants, has amounted to about 340 million dollars. The assistance program has concentrated on agricultural improvement in the Helmand Valley and Land Reclamation Project and on transportation and education.

Once military aid is deducted from the Soviet total, the two donors are about equal in the amount of economic assistance.

The surprising element in the Soviet record is that the Russians have used the influence their aid has given them with remarkable restraint. Afghanistan has not been subjected to Moscow's pressure to alter its policies to suit Soviet international goals. The Russians do not throw their weight around in Kabul or in the outlying areas where they are busy developing the country, probably because they are reasonably sure the United States has no designs on Afghanistan.

This picture of harmonious cooperation in Afghanistan's development naturally could change. The Russians have, although they have not used, an important lever on the Afghan government. Both the army and the air force now are totally dependent on Soviet good will for replacements and spare parts. Soviet military training has understandably influenced the officer corps toward friendship to the U.S.S.R. if not toward imitation.

Part of the price for Afghanistan's freedom from Soviet interference may be its policy of strict neutrality. Dr. Abdul Rawan Farhadi, director of the Political Relations Division of the Foreign Ministry, insisted that "there are absolutely no strings to a single ruble or dollar of aid." But, he said, Afghanistan had refused to join the Organization for Regional Cooperative Development formed by Iran, Turkey, and Pakistan because "it is too close to the Central Treaty Organization," the pact inspired by the United States and directed against the Soviet Union.

178

Leading Afghans from King Mohammed Zahir Shah to the industrious young men in the ministries understand the importance to their country of both Soviet and American aid and of continued cooperation in Afghanistan between the two powers. They are less happy over help from Communist China. This, amounting to about 28 million dollars in the summer of 1967, is devoted to minor aid projects. The Afghan government thoughtfully located all these projects close to Kabul, the capital, so that it would be able without undue exertion to keep a watchful eye on the activities of the Chinese administering the projects.

In Iran and Afghanistan we have two countries steadily developing in the economic and social fields, with the Iranians well ahead. One reason they have been able to advance in conditions of relative political stability is that neither country has yet been affected directly by the emergence of a predatory government in Peking. In the absence of the sort of pressure China has applied to other Asian states, Iran's interests concentrate on the Middle East and western Europe. The Afghans, despite a short common frontier with China, look for economic aid and support to Washington and Moscow.

The Philippine Republic offers a sorry contrast to Iran and Afghanistan. Like them, it is not immediately affected by Chinese expansionism, although Philippine leaders are alert to the potential danger.

But the Philippines seem the prime example in Asia of those states where acute economic difficulties and the corruption, lawlessness, and political immorality these engender have created a situation close to chaos. The reaction of most informed Americans to public manifestations of the country's malaise usually is one of shocked dismay. The shock is all the greater because of the rather complacent attitude with which the majority of Americans approach the islands and their problems, compared to the average American approach to other Asian countries. This country, the visitor thinks, will not be as other former colonial countries, for here the Americans ruled and raised their little brown brothers to democracy and independence.

This euphoria does not last longer than the first view of Manila Bay into which Admiral Dewey sailed all those years ago. Rid yourself of the memories of American schoolmarms who brought enlightment to the boondocks. Forget the line of industrious proconsuls who strove to bring the islands to sovereignty and freedom. Don't raise the question of billions of dollars in direct and indirect aid to Filipinos.

It is all too transparently clear that America failed here, that the present state of the Philippine Republic is worse, not better, than that of comparable states like Malaysia or Thailand. The democratic institutions Americans built are to a painful degree "Potemkin villages," behind which the law of the jungle is too often the only law. Bribery, corruption, nepotism, social injustice are rife. A potentially rich country is rapidly disintegrating economically. The few brave voices raised against the present situation are drowned by the nationalistic oratory of politicians or the blare of jukeboxes in the cafés where the heedless young dance the nights and days away.

The Republic's crisis is the sum of problems so numerous, so interrelated, that it is difficult to seize upon one more significant than the rest. Perhaps one set of statistics will serve as a starting point.

There are 32 million people in the islands today. The population is growing at a rate of 3.2 per cent a year, according to the government's estimate. Other more objective estimates are that the rate is 4 per cent annually. The expectation is that there will be 100 million Filipinos by the turn of the century. No one has made a serious, effective effort to reduce the birth rate. Catholic groups are working on family planning, President

Ferdinand Marcos told me, but their work is still in "the nebulous stage."

As is true elsewhere in Asia, population is only one factor. Food is the other element. But although 60 per cent of the economy is devoted to agriculture, the country does not grow enough food to feed itself.

Rice is the staple of the national diet. But the estimate in the spring of 1967 was that there would be a shortage of 350,000 tons in rice production that year. Sugar, sold mainly to the United States, is a major dollar earner. But sugar production is down. The Filipinos blame this on "natural disasters." Foreign businessmen say that it is the result of inefficiency in the fields and in the mills.

There is much easy optimism in Manila about the future of agriculture, less in the countryside. The government talks about being self-sufficient in rice by 1969, and the spread of IR-8, the miracle rice, first developed at Los Baños in Luzon, gives some ground for confidence. President Marcos talked about a "crash program" to spread the new plant throughout the islands. More fertilizers and pesticides are reaching the farmer. The government's program for increasing irrigation is making some headway.

Against these must be balanced the existence of an almost feudalistic system of land tenure, a legacy, Filipinos say, from the days of Spanish rule. Whatever its origin, the system is remarkably difficult to reform. A land reform bill has been before Congress since 1963.

"Forget it," a foreign technician said. "The big landowners control the Congressmen, and as long as they do no Congress is going to pass the bill." In this expert's view, the landowners would rather take a steady ten-thousand-dollar annual profit from their holdings as they now are than spend another five thousand dollars on improvements to guarantee profits of twenty thousand dollars a few years in the future.

The problem, thus, is not simply that land reform is blocked. It is that the landowners are opposed to those technological improvements that must be made in Philippine agriculture if the country is to support its increasing population.

If the Congress is passive on land reform, it is active in frightening away foreign investment. In consequence the islands' reserves of metals have not been exploited. A case in point is the long negotiations carried on between the government and a European company that wanted to mine the nickel in the island of Mindanao. The Filipinos were not able to make up their minds about the terms of the contract. Meanwhile the European investors noted the increasing emphasis in Congress on expropriation of foreign holdings in the near future. In the end the Europeans closed their brief cases and went home.

Mining is a basic industry. Superficially the outlook is good. But the increase in the value of the country's copper output, for example, has less to do with Philippine initiative and productivity than with the rise in world prices.

Industry made its greatest strides in the early fifties. Since then the situation has deteriorated. What it needs now, according to Sixto Rojas, a young, astute banker, is a rationalization both of the industrial structure itself and of the government agencies dealing with it. There were, he said, too many small factories all making the same products, too many government plans, too much interference by the government and resistance to such interference by industry and agriculture.

The Philippine Gross National Product rose by 4 per cent in 1966. Compare this with Iran's increase of 12 per cent. The economy as it is now organized and administered clearly is not capable of coping with the demands that will be made upon it by an ever-rising population increasingly avid for the luxuries of the American way of life.

Blatant, ubiquitous corruption throughout the government

structure and the police exacerbate economic difficulties. President Marcos admitted to me that when he took office in 1965 he found the customs service "honeycombed with venality." Another, foreign, estimate was that corruption in the customs service was costing the government about 100 million dollars annually in lost revenue.

Bribery is everywhere. "One of the worst aspects of bribery in this country," a columnist wrote in a Manila newspaper, "is that the people who have done nothing wrong bribe to be let alone by people who could abuse them. We have accepted bribery as a way of life. This is our purgatory."

Nepotism and political interference go hand in hand with bribery and graft. Nepotism is not simply a matter of putting a relative into a good government job. In the Philippines it also involves seeing that he stays there, that he is not transferred to another less lucrative post, and that promotion comes regularly. This is not achieved by words alone. Money changes hands.

Political pressures for "jobs for the boys" has resulted in a grossly swollen civil service which is lazy and inefficient to boot. Indeed, one foreign diplomat with long experience in the country believed that the Republic's basic problem was the government's inability to administer itself.

President Marcos, in a gesture much admired by foreigners, dismissed eighty thousand job-holders soon after his inauguration. These same foreigners now sourly admit that probably half that many have been added to the public payroll since.

Bribery, graft, and corruption in underdeveloped countries seem to be governed by rules not found in the United States or western Europe, where bribery, graft, and corruption, after all, are not unknown. The first duty of the politician or civil servant in the emerging countries is to take care of his family. To do otherwise would be to appear a fool as well as an ingrate.

The politician, aiming at re-election, is open to "gifts" from interested industrialists and landowners. The gifts help him finance his campaign. But they also make him attentive to the political wishes of the donors on such matters as tax rebates and land reform. Again, this is a familiar enough story in the West. The difference is that in the Philippines the exchanges are more blatant, this arrogant disregard for what the voters might want more open.

The civil servant thinks of advancement in terms of bribes to superiors. The money used, as often as not, comes from bribes given him for favors, large or small depending on his rank. The whole process, in both politics and bureaucracy, operates in an atmosphere of lighthearted abandonment. The Philippines have to deal with political amorality rather than immorality.

The customs service invariably was singled out as the most corrupt government department in the Philippines. It was there that about 100 million dollars in revenue was lost annually through technical smuggling—that is, the undervaluation or mis-declaration of imports by venal customs officials—and through direct smuggling through the landing of dutiable items such as foreign cigarettes over distant beaches.

The President claimed that his efforts have reduced the volume of cigarette smuggling by 60 per cent and that customs collections had risen by 42 per cent. The smuggling of "warm bodies"—illegal Chinese immigrants—had been eliminated, he said.

The blatant, disastrous corruption of the Philippines consti-tutes a very real danger in a country already in serious economic straits and with a turbulent political record. Already, the spread of corruption has led to a breakdown of law and order on a staggering scale.

Mayor James Gordon, American-born but a naturalized Fili-pino, was shot dead in his office in the city hall of Olongapo because he had refused to pay tribute to the gangs that run brothels and gambling in his city. Olongapo is near the United States naval base at Subic Bay. When the fleet's in, the money comes in with it, and one moderate estimate is that the sailors spend "at least a million" in Olongapo during their leave.

Lawlessness has spread from Manila to the most remote islands. In the capital the rich and the well-to-do live in suburbs that are, in fact if not in name, fortified villages. Girt by high stone walls, these suburbs are guarded by private security guards who check every entry and patrol the walls. The rich and even the moderately well-to-do cannot depend on either the city police or the constabulary, notoriously underpaid and vulnerable to bribery.

Meanwhile, in the remote islands, pirates in fast motorboats land from the sea, hold the police at bay, and rob shops and the homes of the rich.

Violence has become a way of life. I asked a friend how many Filipinos carried a pistol. "Every male that can afford one," he said. "You see, with us it's a mark of virility."

The gravity of these two linked situations, corruption and lawlessness, is compounded by another: the social irresponsibility of the rich. This is not confined to the major landowners' opposition to agricultural reform and improvement. It shows itself in a certain aristocratic disdain for the problems of the country, a complacent belief that the politicians will stay bought, that the people will forever be content to be gulled and tricked by the politicians and scorned by the rich.

This attitude on the part of the upper crust irritates hard-working aid officials.

"My God, I heard about a party the other night," one said, "they told me it cost fifteen thousand dollars, a band from Hong Kong, champagne, gold favors for the girls. Dresses costing four hundred dollars. I know a village you could feed for five years on the money spent for that one party. Jesus, won't these rich people here ever wake up?"

The answer at the moment seems to be "no." Unless the rapid deterioration of the situation is arrested, the Republic inevitably will move into one of those periods of political turmoil in which salvation appears possible only through extreme measures. The sophisticated reader may consider that the present situation has been exaggerated; after all, corruption is endemic in Asia, violence and lawlessness the natural consequence of a period in which one sort of rule, colonialism, has disappeared and another, national independence, has not taken strong roots. My reply is that nowhere in nearly thirty years as a foreign correspondent have I seen corruption as unashamed as that in Manila; I felt far safer walking the streets of Saigon or Vientiane at night than I did in the Philippine capital.

In such situations, there always is a tendency to pin hopes on an individual rather than a system. President Ferdinand Marcos has all the outer attributes of the strong man. He is only fifty, he is energetic, and he is brave; his bravery, in fact, is part of the history of his country. He talks like a statesman and a patriot. Yet the President is the victim of a perversion of government that is powerful enough to prevent him carrying out the very measures—land reform, for example—that he knows are indispensable to finding a way out of the morass.

The second time I saw him, some thousands of peasants had been brought in from the countryside to proclaim their faith in Marcos and to demonstrate in support of his policies. There were buses streaming toward the Malacanang Palace "as far as the eye can see," as an exultant presidential aide pointed out. There were cheers, banners, impassioned speeches. It was all outwardly impressive and basically phony.

These toughened, work-weary farmers are not the voice of government in the Philippines. That voice comes from the families of industrialists and landowners who control Congress and the press. Unless *those* voices are raised in favor of reform, a contingency more remote than Premier Kosygin calling for free speech, President Marcos can do no more than nibble at the outside of the problem.

The man deserves better than that. Perhaps because inwardly he senses the implacability of the opposition on internal progress and his consequent inability to act, he is deeply concerned with international issues. No head of government in Asia is more anxious than he to take advantage of the turmoil aroused in China by the Cultural Revolution. This is the time, he told me, to "accelerate the planning of a united Asia.

"Asia's principal political-military problem," he said, is "to organize and equalize the military force of Red China which is the central factor in Asian politics. No one nation or group of nations now can hope to equal the power of the Chinese. That's why we need SEATO."

The President conceded the difficulty of establishing any general political alliance that was anti-Communist in basic intent while Cambodia and Burma maintain their precarious neutrality and Japan's movement toward participation stops short of political involvement in that sort of grouping.

"These conditions will change," he predicted. "One factor will be the coming American and Allied victory in South Vietnam. Another is the ousting of a Communist regime in Indonesia. A third may be the end of an organized central government in China. Peking's influence on other countries and its ability to threaten already has been reduced by the Cultural Revolution. The time has come for Asians to act together."

This is a bolder approach than most Asian leaders were prepared to follow in 1967. It is evidence of a more realistic view of the continent's long-term problems than most are willing to take. It is also, I fear, well ahead of its time. Yet the movement toward regionalism in Asia cannot be discounted merely because it is sporadic and held up by national rivalries. Two World Wars were required to move Western Europe toward unity. The Asians, with the European example before them and China's implacable belligerency dinned into their ears by every Peking broadcast, may find it possible to move faster.

Despite President Marcos's high aspirations for his country and his broad and farsighted approach to Asian regionalism, one left the Philippines with a sense of impending disaster.

Among foreigners the commonest prediction was that the Marcos Administration or its successor, finding it impossible to deal with the country's problems in the presence of a hostile Congress and an inefficient, corrupt officialdom, would attempt to install an authoritarian regime of the right that would govern by decree. Committed to action against both economic and social problems, this regime would render Congress powerless and seek to clean up bribery, graft, and corruption. Repeatedly the visitor is told, "Only a dictator can clean up this mess."

There is a fundamental error in this prognosis. It supposes that the people most hostile to reform in the essentials of economic and social life would support an authoritarian government devoted to reform. There might be minor easements for the poor, as, indeed, there were in the early days of the Third Reich. But economic power would remain in familiar hands and the drive for reform would be diverted to less dangerous sectors.

Something much more serious than an imitation of the Spanish or Portuguese dictatorships, however, may well develop in the Philippines if things continue as they are. The present poverty, the inequalities of wealth, the absence of social justice, the lawlessness, and the corruption are the stuff upon which Communists feed. It is significant that in 1967, as the national condition grew worse, the Hukbalahap movement returned to vigorous life in the countryside. In the fifties this Marxist guerrilla movement challenged the government's rule over wide areas. Eventually it was crushed. But it was dormant, not dead. Now, as things grow worse for the peasant, the Huks can rely on him for the information, the food, the shelter on which such movements live.

It is easy enough to discount the Huk movement, as many diplomats do, by terming it a sort of Philippine Mafia interested more in money and loot than in politics. Such an attitude presupposes that the Huks will remain as they are at present. Unfortunately, history provides us with no such easy assurances.

The combination of the Huks—with their arms, their discipline, their kinship with the people and the countryside—and the prevalent economic malaise, corruption, and lawlessness offers communism a great opportunity. If economic conditions continue to deteriorate and the social evils to which they are tied continue to prosper, the United States must expect a dangerous period of turmoil in the islands.

If we are learning anything about Asia, it surely is that its people respond very much as do those in the West. If there is economic opportunity and it is explained to them, they will seize it. If new methods in agriculture are proved to be better, they will use them. If the old and the new can be balanced within the framework of accepted tradition, they will be accepted.

But if government does not respond to the people's needs and wishes, if the drift toward economic and social chaos continues, if the rich get richer and the poor get poorer, we must be prepared for trouble. In all considerations of that trouble, it is worth reckoning the value of a successful War of National Liberation in the Philippines to the Communists: American bases endangered, the United States flouted and shamed in the nation it raised to independence, and, strategically, the islands that are the southern anchor of the American position along Asia's eastern seaboard turned over to strife.

Here it would seem is another reason why the present battle

189

against the Communists' War of National Liberation in South Vietnam must be won and be seen to be won by the watchers in every Asian capital.

In assessing where the Asians stand now, and what this means and does not mean for Americans and their policy in Asia, the developing position of the Republic of Indonesia is an important factor. When the elements that have slowed Communist expansion in Asia are considered, the bloody dismissal of the pro-Communist rulers of Indonesia has an important place. Again, there is a relationship between this and the other seminal events in Asia: the Cultural Revolution in China and the United States military intervention to save South Vietnam. Only the historian of the future will be able to assign the correct weight to each; for the moment it is perhaps sufficient to say that what happened in Indonesia strengthened the determination of anti-Communists throughout Southeast Asia to resist the imposition of Communist rule.

The massacre of the Communists in 1965—at least three hundred thousand were killed—was a grisly object lesson for Asia. For the first time since the end of colonialism, a people had risen against a Communist regime and eliminated it. Predictably, many of the vengeful Indonesians were animated by compulsions other than pure anticommunism. But the lesson remained: Communist regimes and parties are not invincible; revolution is more effective an answer than resignation.

The effects of the Indonesian action extended far beyond the country's ten thousand islands and 107 million people. The "confrontation" between Malaysia and the British on one hand and President Sukarno's forces was ended by Djakarta. Foreign Minister Adam Malik has since been busily trying to construct a regional grouping, including the ex-enemy Malaysia, that would have as its chief if publicly unstated objective the checking of Communist Chinese expansion in Southeast Asia.

Meanwhile Indonesia has re-entered the United Nations. General Suharto, the Acting President, has solicited trade and aid from the western powers, considered neocolonialist demons by Sukarno. Theoretically the new Indonesia under Suharto follows an active and independent foreign policy—that is, a neutralist policy. Actually its present neutralism tends to be western in sympathy rather than Communist as it was in the past.

Indonesia's relations with Communist China deteriorated steadily from the time of the massacre because the Indonesian Communists were strongly influenced and often advised by the Chinese Communists through their embassy in Djakarta. By late 1967 diplomatic relations had reached the breaking point. Simultaneously the new regime began to turn to the United Nations for help. The Johnson Administration agreed to provide one third of the approximately 200 million dollars Indonesia needed to cover the gap between her export revenues and her import requirements. At the same time the United States pumped 2 million dollars into the country in the form of spare parts for army machinery used for road repair and drainage projects in West and East Java.

Throughout Southeast Asia, from Manila to Burma, "new" Indonesian diplomats made it clear that their government's abrupt change in policy was to be permanent. Almost overnight Communist China has replaced the United States as Indonesia's enemy.

What should concern Americans now is not the present depth of this anti-Communist sentiment, which certainly appears genuine, but the durability of the Suharto government. The General became Acting President at a time of national euphoria excited by the overthrow of the Communists. Since then he has had to deal with the multiple economic and social problems left behind by Sukarno. To date he has not been significantly successful.

General Suharto's goals are deceptively simple: a balanced budget, the first since the country became independent of the Dutch, austerity for both government and people, and the return to civilian government. No sensible Indonesian official quarrels with the wisdom of this program. But many see its political vulnerability. It is a drab bread-and-water policy for a highly volatile people that for nearly twenty years has been fed on the raw meat and firewater of "Bung" Sukarno's political histrionics.

Criticism of his program in the bureaucracy and public restiveness over austerity seems to have increased Suharto's obsession with secrecy and his tendency, always strong, to concentrate the decision-making power in his own hands. At the same time he goes out of his way to discourage the idea that he intends to remain as a military dictator by emphasizing the virtues of civilian and military cooperation and of normal political life.

The latter seems further from achievement than the former. Most politicians on the national and local level are men trained and influenced in the Sukarno days. They are not attracted by the more sober approach of the new regime. Foreign Minister Adam Malik has attempted with only limited success to build a left-wing secular party. The efforts of Vice-President Mohammed Hatta to construct a moderate Moslem group incurred General Suharto's wrath, and the idea was dropped.

Echoes of the grumbling against the regime were audible in every Southeast Asian capital, but especially in Singapore. Many of the Chinese of that city were still shaken by the murder of so many of their compatriots in Indonesia and the eviction of so many others who were not Communists but simply Chinese. The Singapore Chinese spent no time mourning the massacred Communists; their concern was that Malay racism, inflamed by the belief that every Chinese was a Communist and anti-Moslem, might spread among the peoples of Malaysia and the Philippines. The Indonesian students, who played an important role in maintaining Sukarno in power and an equally important part in his eventual defeat, by the middle of 1967 were again beginning to demonstrate against what they considered the "antidemocratic" actions of the new government. General Suharto's only known response was a comment that the students, the outlawed Communists, and the moderate politicians all were elements in the same plot to divert him and his colleagues from the rejuvenation of Indonesia.

Despite such grumbling, General Suharto's political accomplishments are solid and evident. The Communists are beaten, their leaders dead, their communication with Peking interrupted. Indonesian foreign policy has switched from profitless adventure to cooperation with neighbors in the construction of a firm political alliance in Southeast Asia. Unfortunately the regime's economic underpinning remains shaky; recovery has been all too slow.

Although every Asian country, not excluding Japan and Iran, faces economic problems, nowhere do these appear as overwhelming as in Indonesia. For there the usual problems of developing the country, difficult in themselves, have been compounded by the insane spending on prestige projects of the Sukarno regime. Under the circumstances its successors have been forced to spend more time rescuing than building. The situation in Indonesia forcibly recalls that of Ghana, after Kwame Nkrumah was ousted. In both cases a military regime pledged to austerity and direct action took over and found itself struggling in a morass of debt, shortages, and economic disarray.

Indonesia's economic maladies begin with the overpopulation of the island of Java, unemployment and underemployment throughout the Republic's ten-thousand-odd tropical islands, inaccessible natural resources, decrepit transport and communications systems, industries near ruin from inefficient management, a desperate shortage of technical and managerial abilities, a swollen bureaucracy that, in common with others in Asia, is shockingly underpaid, and, finally, the chief legacy of President Sukarno's economic insanities, a staggering load of debts.

All this in a country that was considered, on independence, to possess one of the solidest economic bases in Asia. But Sukarno the Liberator became Sukarno the Wrecker. Financial mismanagement resulted in budget deficits twice the size of the government revenue. In 1966 inflation rocketed in one period at the rate of more than 400 per cent a *day!* The best that government economists could hope for in 1967 was to limit inflation to about 100 per cent for the year.

The first object of the Suharto government and its chief economics adviser, Dr. Widjojo Nitisastro, under these conditions was to institute fiscal austerity, direct the economy toward provision of adequate food, clothing, and other consumer goods, and cut funds for the government's prestige projects. Some success had been recorded by the summer of 1967. Prices for rice and textiles stabilized. There was a fall, small but appreciable, in the cost of living index over a two-week period in May. Nevertheless exports—and Indonesia, like other primary producers in Asia, lives by exports—failed to thrive as expected.

Meanwhile the government began to return to former owners the businesses and industrial plants expropriated, under the sacred name of nationalization, by Sukarno and his merry men. Tire, shoe, and pharmaceutical factories began to operate again on sensible lines under their original owners. Foreign interests were invited to prospect for offshore oil and Indonesia's timber resources opened to foreign companies.

The effects on Indonesia's millions of peasants were minimal. Agriculture from rice to rubber received little actual attention under Sukarno. Indonesia's rubber plantations have not benefited from research and development as have those of neighboring Malaysia; generally the Indonesian product is inferior to the Malaysian. Rice, the staple food, still is cultivated with antiquated methods. In the Celebes, the rice granary, the crop rots because sea transport to carry it to the other islands is so expensive that the price in the markets is prohibitive. In the hills of West Sumatra, the crop goes unharvested because the roads over which it should be transported to the ports are impassable. There is a general shortage of fertilizer, pesticides, and modern agricultural equipment. The new, improved strains of rice are only now being belatedly introduced.

The export of copra is complicated by exorbitant costs for shipping that can quadruple the price. The handling of any export is delayed by the bureaucracy which, although no more venal than others in Asia, insists on a staggering amount of paper work and signatures before a cargo can be cleared. In some cases thirty-nine different signatures are required for a single item.

Within the over-all economic problem lies a major social problem whose solution will affect Indonesia's prospects for recovery. This is the future of the three million Chinese in Indonesia. The Chinese began to settle in the country seven hundred years ago. In Indonesia, as elsewhere in Southeast Asia, they prospered as bankers, businessmen, and merchants. Just over a million Chinese businessmen until recently dominated the country's retail trade.

The extirpation of the Indonesian Communist Party, directed from Peking, sounded the alarm. The Chinese since have been accused of financing and sympathizing with the party. They are hated by the Malays as rich foreigners who have gulled the honest, unsuspecting Malays and profited enormously at the expense of the country's Malay majority. Moslem students attack Chinese homes. Local officials levy illegal and punitive fines on small Chinese communities. The Chinese are caught between a desire to remain in the only land they know and the fear that, if they do, their lives will be made miserable or may even be forfeited.

The seriousness of this problem came home one morning in Singapore when I was talking to Prime Minister Lee Kuan Yew. Another boatload of Chinese fleeing Indonesia had arrived that morning.

"What can we do?" he asked. "There are too many people in Singapore already. But they are in a pitiable condition, pitiable. We let them rest, feed them, and give them funds to go on—to Hong Kong or to China. People who were not Communists, people who worked hard all their lives. But they felt they had to leave."

Indonesia's Chinese problem in essentials is no different from that of Malaysia. But there, enlightened efforts by both the Malays and the Chinese have brought about a division of governmental and economic responsibility that works fairly well, and the Chinese willingly support the Malaysian government's efforts to raise living standards among the Malay masses. Indonesia is a long way from this. The fear among overseas Chinese elsewhere in Southeast Asia is that General Suharto's regime will exploit anti-Chinese sentiment and thus divert attention from the economic difficulties that will face the country for many years to come.

Asia, we in the West too often tell ourselves, is full of impossibles. The Asians do not see it that way. To the western mind the spectacle of General Suharto, intellectually limited regular soldier, presiding over the efforts to restore a scattered, disparate people to unity and progress seems doomed to failure, an impossibility. The Indonesians, however, despite many a happy gibe at the General's New Order, consider Suharto's character and determination far more important than the extent of his acquaintance with John Stuart Mill or John Kenneth Galbraith.

For every Indonesian I interviewed in Asia placed the maximum importance on unselfish, single-minded leadership. They were not particularly concerned about General Suharto's views on western-style democracy. They were concerned about the General's ability to mobilize Indonesia for a great national effort aimed at nothing less than survival.

"Democracy can come later," a young Indonesian diplomat said in Manila. "Now we have to eat."

No one can be optimistic about the Philippines or Indonesia, just as no one now should be pessimistic about Iran and Afghanistan. Each of the first two has to find its own way out of an incredibly complicated economic and social labyrinth. The difference between the two is that, for the moment, Indonesia has a strong-willed if limited leader who knows what he wants and has the power to get it, and the Philippine Republic has a strong, intelligent, competent President whose ability to act is severely restricted by purchasable Congressmen, a corrupt and inefficient civil service, and an upper class largely unconcerned by anything in a changing world that does not contribute to its pleasure or profit.

General Suharto's advantage is that the group that ruined his country and directed it toward vassalage to the Chinese Communists has been eliminated. President Marcos must do the best he can with what he has at hand. Under present conditions it is highly unlikely that he or any successor working under the same conditions can avert disaster for the Philippines.

IX

Asia, America, and the Future

Asia's dazzling variety, that can encompass a country as stable politically as Malaysia and one as chaotic as South Vietnam, that numbers the boisterously belligerent Afridis and the docile Ceylonese among its peoples, bewilders the visitor until he begins to realize that from Tokyo to Teheran two seminal problems link all Asia: the age-old contest between the rise in population and the productivity of agriculture, and the existence in the center of this continent of the great Chinese people. Some authorities, usually for the very best of reasons, attempt to ignore the second in considering the first. This dangerously nonsensical view is possible, one fears, only to those who live among the mandarins of the Secretariat of the United Nations.

Any sensible projection of Asia's future must accept the possibility that a failure by agriculture to keep pace with the demand for food will certainly provide the Chinese with a splendid opportunity to do exactly what they have said they wish to do: organize the rural masses in communism against the developed states, which are dominated, in Peking's mythology, by the United States and, for the time being, the "revisionists" ruling the Soviet Union.

One of the most extraordinary and perhaps, in a less dangerous period, endearing traits of Americans is their refusal to believe that other people, steadily and seriously plotting the downfall of the Republic, can be foolish enough to divulge their tactics. Just as the British, with the exception of the valiant few led by Winston Churchill, refused to take Adolf Hitler's *Mein Kampf* seriously, so few Americans have listened to the warning blatantly announced by the Chinese Communists in 1965.

An article published in all major Chinese newspapers on

198

September 3 and written by Marshal Lin Piao, Mao Tse-tung's Defense Minister and putative heir, outlined Chinese strategy. Here is a lesson that all should read, Republican or Democrat, conservative or liberal, black or white. For it concerns not the national policy of China but a prescription for international chaos. Nothing I saw or heard in Asia contradicted my belief that this article is and will be for years to come the blueprint for Chinese policy for Asia.

Tomorrow Marshal Lin Piao and Chairman Mao may be replaced by Defense Minister Wu and Chairman Lee. But as long as China remains a dynamic country under communism, the remainder of Asia will have to cope with the strategy and tactics similar to those outlined by Marshal Lin.

When the article was published, American attention fixed on the Marshal's comments on the Vietnam war. Superficially these comments were important; actually they said nothing:

> The determination of the Chinese people to support and aid the Vietnamese people in their struggle against U.S. aggression and for national salvation is unshakable. No matter what U.S. imperialism may do to expand its war adventure, the Chinese people will do everything in their power to support the Vietnamese people until every single one of the U.S. aggressors is driven out of Vietnam.

Good full-blooded stuff, this. But, as the observant will notice, no cheer for the Vietnamese beyond an expression of Chinese determination to give support and aid. What should concern Americans when they consider Asia, especially Southeast Asia, are the longer passages on the dimensions of the struggle Communist China endorses and foments.

> It must be emphasized that Comrade Mao Tse-tung's theory of the establishment of rural revolutionary base areas and the encirclement of cities from the countryside is of outstanding and universal practical importance for the present revolutionary

struggle of all the oppressed nations and peoples, and particularly for the revolutionary struggles of the oppressed nations and
peoples in Asia, Africa, and Latin America against imperialism
and its lackeys.

Many countries and peoples in Asia, Africa, and Latin America are now being subjected to aggression and enslavement on a
serious scale by the United States and their lackeys. The basic
political and economic conditions in many of these countries have
many similarities to those that prevailed in old China.

As in China, the peasant question is extremely important in
these regions. The peasants constitute the main force of the
national-democratic revolution against the imperialists and their
lackeys.

In committing aggression against these countries, the imperialists usually begin by seizing the big cities and the main lines of
communications, but they are unable to bring the vast countryside completely under their control. The countryside, and the
countryside alone, can provide the broad areas in which the
revolutionaries can maneuver freely.

The countryside, and the countryside alone, can provide the
revolutionary bases from which the revolutionaries can go forward to final victory. Precisely for this reason, Comrade Mao
Tse-tung's theory of establishing revolutionary base areas in the
rural districts and encircling the cities from the countryside is
attracting more and more attention among the peoples in these
regions.

Now come the guts of the argument:

Taking the entire globe, if North America and Western Europe
can be called the "cities of the world," then Asia, Africa, and
Latin America constitute "the rural areas of the world." Since
World War II the proletarian revolutionary movement has for
various reasons been temporarily held back in the North American and West European capitalist countries, while the people's
revolutionary movement in Asia, Africa, and Latin America has
been growing vigorously. In a sense, the contemporary world

revolution also presents a picture of the encirclement of cities by the rural areas.

No one can complain that he has not been warned. And warned by a people whose view of history and its developments is even longer than that of the Russians. Those who read and ponder these paragraphs and consider the course of Wars of National Liberation in Asia must conclude that Chinese hostility toward the West and support for dissidents is far deeper than the rather jejune maxims of Chairman Mao. This is danger: for ourselves, for our children, for our children's children.

Now it can be argued that the Chinese have never done more than talk about this conflict between the rural and urban areas of the world, just as they have never done anything more, at this writing, about physical aid to the Vietnamese in terms of manpower, than talk about it. The argument misses the point. The Chinese have told us how they see a world struggle developing and that we and our lackeys are cast in the role of ultimate victims.

Any analysis of what the Chinese and *their* lackeys are doing and how it is regarded by Asian nations should be prefaced by some estimate of the Chinese. Although I tried three times to obtain a visa to the People's Republic, I never came close to a visa. This estimate, therefore, must be based on my talks with overseas Chinese and with those, luckier than I, who had been given a guided tour of the Middle Kingdom.

On this basis which, unfortunately, is the only one an objective American is likely to achieve, I think we should begin by considering the notion, so prevalent among Sinophobes and, latterly, among those who oppose American policy in Asia, that the Chinese, by some quick mutation, have become a bewilderingly competent people. No one will contest that they are an old people, that they have a tradition of scholarship and literature extending back beyond the time when the British were painting themselves blue in caves, that they invented everything from the rudder to gunpowder.

Equally, no one can or should deny that the Chinese are capable of great cruelty, that they enjoy a sense of racial and national superiority beside which the French appear blushing violets, and that they assume a Heaven-sent right to rule such territories contiguous to China as they consider important.

Of course, we are told the Chinese are basically a peaceful people. We might remember that Kamikaze, the Divine Wind of the Japanese, was first used to describe a gale that destroyed a Chinese fleet sailing for Japan.

Because they are distant, numerous, and, to use a favorite Victorian word, inscrutable, we tend to take the Chinese at their own valuation. Wiseacres at dinner parties announce that since the Chinese "invented" guerrilla warfare it is a mistake to attempt to fight them or their pupils. The Chinese are no better and no worse at guerrilla warfare than the Portuguese and Spanish who harassed Napoleon's marshals in the Iberian Peninsula or the farmers who picked off Gage's troops at Lexington and Concord. It is worth remembering, too, that Communist China's chief contribution to modern warfare has been the Human Wave attack, a tactic about as subtle as a charging rhinoceros.

In Asia I met Chinese of every class who were intelligent, humane, and courteous, but no more so than Pakistanis or Laotians or Filipinos. I saw nothing, except for the fact that there are a great many of them, to make me believe that the Chinese hold the master keys to the future or that they were any more or any less than the Germans of 1940 or the Russians of 1947. They pull their pants on one leg at a time. To picture them as a mysterious national force to be appeased is an insult to the American intelligence. But we will always find academicians and intellectuals to paint this picture, just as some of their predecessors saw the Nazis and the Italian Fascists as the wave of the future and the Stalinist Communists as a second such wave.

Communist China aspires, as Marshal Lin's paragraphs show, to the leadership of the rural areas of Asia. Why, then, has she failed so far?

In the case of Japan, of course, she never had a hope. For Japan, although not linked to North America and Western Europe by Marshal Lin, is a city, not a rural area. Her economic revival, encouraged by the United States, and a long period of relative social and economic stability have removed her from the scope of China's immediate ambitions. But there are other Asian countries that definitely belong in the Chinese category of rural areas, which have rejected Chinese Communist subversion, either overt or covert. Malaysia, with British help, fought a long and costly was against Chinese guerrillas. Thailand is now combatting a guerrilla force inspired and partially armed by China. Both these countries have developed their economies without communism; both are resolutely opposed to it. Perhaps they see things more clearly in Kuala Lumpur and Bangkok than in New York or London or Paris. People there, including overseas Chinese, do not see liberation and a great popular revolutionary movement in Chinese policy; they see chaos, servitude, and death.

Whatever the Chinese say about the United States, and they assail it night and day in every tongue of Asia, a gratifying number of Asians refuse to believe that the United States is in Asia, militarily or in any other sense, including aid, for the object of subjecting the Asian peoples. Not all of them like Americans, naturally. Most of them will be glad to see our backs. But they resolutely refuse to accept the Chinese version of the American presence.

What is perhaps more important is that a steadily increasing number of ordinary Asians—peasants, small shopkeepers, minor officials in remote country villages—have come to understand that the American presence usually means help in the things they need most, whether it is a new way to grow rice or protection against the guerrillas whose extortions go beyond anything they recall from colonial times. When these people express these views to visitors they are not being pro-American; they are talking sheer common sense. They need help and they know it. "The long noses," "the white eyes," provide the help.

This book deals with the present and the military situation in the Indo-Chinese peninsula that has brought the American military to that area. But even if there were no wars, if Laos, Thailand, and South Vietnam lived in peace, there would still be a need for an American presence, economic and political, in Asia. For the Chinese challenge and Chinese ambitions are enduring; independent governments moving very slowly toward democracy in Asia are China's political rivals, and every peasant who turns from subsistence farming to a modest profit on his crop is Mao Tse-tung's unknown enemy.

No, the United States would not be done with Asia even if the war were to end tomorrow. For the older war between people and food must be won by the people of Asia with American help before their freedom can be considered safe from China. If they lose that war, and they may if there is no American help, then eventually communism will win. Some Americans are quick to say, "Well, let it; there's nothing we can do about it."

The Asians don't see it that way. They won't have communism. And they believe that there is a great deal we can do about it. Here the basic argument is one adumbrated earlier: unless the economies of these countries are improved to the point of self-sufficiency in food, the Communists will exploit misery and take over these rural areas. Again the urban intellectual may shrug his shoulders. It is quite possible he will take another view if Malaysia goes, or Burma or India.

AMERICA'S STAKE IN ASIA

American policy in Asia must embrace two objectives. First the United States must prevent the North Vietnamese from taking over South Vietnam in what the Communists would then claim as a victorious War of National Liberation. The second objective is to guide and encourage the economies to the point where, once the wars are over, the governments and the peoples are in a position to resist Chinese subversion.

Earlier in this book I emphasized the effect of China's Cultural Revolution on Chinese influence in Southeast Asia. The Cultural Revolution is an unexpected dividend for American policy in Asia. But there is no guarantee that it will last forever and no assurance that the government that eventually succeeds that of Chairman Mao and Marshal Lin will be less aggressive. Indeed, we must consider that any new regime might seek to consolidate its internal position by supporting another War of National Liberation, possibly in greater seriousness than the Chinese are now supporting the North Vietnamese.

Again, we will be warned that such a supposition is at odds with Chinese character. Is it?

In July 1967, when the Cultural Revolution was at its height, Communist China emerged as the sponsor of two of Southeast Asia's most important Communist parties, the Indonesian and the Burmese. The action reflected the continuing dynamism of the parent party. For the Indonesian party had been almost eliminated by the bloodletting that attended the supplanting of Sukarno and, as we have seen, all Chinese in Indonesia subsequently were suspected of supporting and financing the party and of secretly sympathizing with its revival. Nevertheless the Peking leadership restated its support. The Burmese party, operating in a country theoretically devoted to neutralism, got Chinese endorsement at the moment when relations between the two governments were severely strained and a less aggressive attitude in Peking might have dictated prudence.

205

Both these parties won Peking's favor by committing themselves to the Maoist line in international communism and by declaring their hostility to the Russian party's "revisionism."

There were other examples of Peking's continuing interest in overseas Communist parties. At a time when Chairman Mao and his colleagues faced rebellion in some sections of the People's Army and serious dissidence in at least five provinces of mainland China, Peking emphasized its support and approval of Communist movements in Thailand, Laos, and the Philippines. It called a Communist-inspired peasant uprising in Nawalbari in northeast India "a spark of Chairman Mao Tse-tung's thought glowing on Indian soil."

That venerable arsonist, however, appeared chiefly interested in proclaiming his support for the battered Indonesian party then operating, to a very limited degree, underground. Peking made it clear that the party would have its support for what it was worth and, in announcing this, went to some lengths to emphasize the satellite relationship of the party to big brother on the mainland.

Relations between the Chinese and General Ne Win, a crusty character, had deteriorated steadily through the first half of the year. The Burmese government, affronted by Chinese subversion, reacted in a manner customary in Asia. Students—one wonders if Asian students ever study—and urban idlers set upon Chinese residents. They apparently needed little prompting. The Chinese, alone of the foreigners who once ran Burma's trade, have survived almost unscathed, and, as elsewhere in Asia, they are regarded as usurers and profiteers taking advantage of the honest Burmese. The attacks on the Chinese prompted the customary denunciation of General Ne Win's government by Peking.

As that most astute of China watchers, Tilman Durdin, pointed out, there was a degree of difference in Peking's attitude to the two vassal parties.

Chairman Mao's principal press organ *Hung Chi* (Red Flag) said that the Chinese Communist Party firmly supported the Indonesian party in its campaign to overthrow the "fascist" regime of General Suharto. In the case of Burma, *Jenmin Jih Pao,* the official organ of the Chinese party, denounced General Ne Win's government as a "traitorous, dictatorial, warlord regime," an agent of American imperialism and Soviet revisionism. But there was no pledge of support for the Burmese party.

This could mean that the Chinese leadership still retains hopes of leading General Ne Win in the direction it chooses. Or it may indicate that Chairman Mao, recognizing the splits within the Burmese party and the weakness of its aging leader, Thakin Than Tun, regards it as a bad bet at present.

This Chinese solicitude for distant parties should emphasize one element in the situation in Southeast Asia of maximum importance to the United States. The Cultural Revolution and the American intervention in Southeast Asia have bought a breathing space for the other countries in the area. But the Chinese have not been entirely diverted from their interest in arousing the rural areas against the "cities" by their internal convulsions, and, unless the battle for food can be won, their opportunities will increase.

How goes that battle? In other chapters we have watched its progress in individual countries. By October 1967 the Food and Agriculture Organization of the United Nations had prepared as accurate an estimate as was possible in view of the circumstances in the Far East. It said:

> After decreasing by about 2 per cent in 1965, agricultural production in the Far East, excluding China (mainland) is estimated to have increased by 3 per cent in 1966. In both years

rice production was the main determinant, dropping by about 10 per cent in 1965 and recovering in 1966 to about the same level as the year before. India's food situation continued to pose severe problems, since rains again failed in 1966. The country's production of food-grains (including pulses) which fell to 72,000,000 tons in 1965 is estimated as only 73–75,000,000 tons in 1966 in comparison with the 88,000,000 tons needed to feed the population. Pakistan also suffered from drought and food-grain production declined by 1,500,000 tons in 1966.

Rice production recovered in Ceylon, Indonesia, Japan, Republic of Korea, the Philippines, and Thailand in 1966 but there were shortfalls in Burma, Cambodia, Pakistan, and the Republic of Vietnam. Wheat production decreased by 12 per cent in 1966, with sharp reductions in India, Japan, and Pakistan. The region's sugar production appears to have declined. . . .

This somber outlook must be considered in the light of the failure thus far of most Asian governments to cope with population growth. In India and Pakistan, as we saw, the best that can be said is that the governments are keenly alive to the problem and that a start has been made. Singapore is the exception. But the Lion City's population is a minor factor in Asia's tragic growth. Think of the projected populations for 1970: India, 542,575,000; Pakistan, 129,295,000; Burma, 27,585,000; Thailand, 35,685,000. Remember, too, that from Japan west only a few countries have embarked seriously and thoroughly on programs for increased agricultural productivity. Taiwan may be the only underdeveloped country in the Far East, perhaps in the world, where agricultural production is outpacing population growth. From 1950 through 1965, annual agricultural output on that island increased at an average rate of 5 per cent. This rate has slowed somewhat in the last two years but it is still well ahead of population growth, now estimated at 2.7 per cent annually.

The harsh truth, however, is that, if conditions remain as they are, the battle to produce enough food to feed Asia's new mouths will be lost. Continued and expanded United States technical assistance will be necessary in agriculture and associated fields, if America does not wish to see this deteriorating situation turned to the advantage of the Communists and to the distress of its friends and allies in Asia. This will be a burden, although a far lighter one than continued military assistance in the future to independent governments fighting to stifle Wars of National Liberation fomented by the Chinese among hungry populations. Those wars may be prevented, if Asia can feed herself.

The emphasis in Asia has been on rice because, in the next ten years, world demand for it will grow faster than for any other cereal. Assuming that prices remain relatively stable and incomes rise by 1985, according to the Food and Agriculture Organization of the United Nations, world demand will show an increase of 100 million tons over the demand in the years 1961–65.

"It seems certain," the FAO reported, "that the world will not be able to grow enough rice to satisfy its needs unless full use is made of available resources."

Finally, it must be kept in mind that, even in those countries where the rate of population increase can be kept within reasonable limits, the improvement in living standards means more rice for home consumption and less for export, a condition that is expected to apply in Thailand before the end of this decade.

These are the dimensions of the problem. What must be done to solve it by Asians with whatever help the United States and the rest of the developed world can provide? We have glimpsed how individual governments in Asia are attacking the food-population issue. A general survey of prospects must emphasize certain essentials.

There is a scarcity of land resources for expanded rice cultivation. Thus the emphasis must be on increasing productivity in those countries, such as Burma and Thailand, where the population pressure is not as intense as in, say, East Pakistan. Average rice yields per acre in the Far East are probably only half of what they could be if modern methods of technology were applied.

To improve the cultivation of existing acreage there must be more fertilizers, improved varieties of rice, better control of pests and diseases, a more economic use of draft animals, and more water available for the farmer. Massive schemes like the Mekong River project will take years to complete. The Asian farmer cannot wait for years.

The most important single element in progress, however, will be the increase in economic incentives: the transformation of a subsistence agriculture into a commercial operation. The successes scored in this field in Japan, Taiwan, and, to a lesser degree in Thailand, show what can be done, but generally the record in the Far East is disappointing. The farmer still needs better systems of farm credit, better marketing organization, new systems of land tenure, and financial arrangements that will give him better access to the fertilizers, pesticides, new rice strains, and tools he needs if productivity is to rise. It is impossible to believe that a program of this size and complexity can be carried to a successful conclusion in the Far East, and economic hardship and political instability averted, without the massive help of the United States.

Unfortunately this situation is developing in the Far East at the same time that Americans seem to be coming progressively less interested in their responsibilities for the future of Asia. Indeed, there seems to be a very good chance that in the near future a wave of neo-isolationism will spread across the country and that its principal targets will be those areas, Asia, Latin America, and Africa, where America has given much and, to the average man, received little more in return than kicks and insults. The same, of course, could be said of certain European countries.

Happily this may not endure, first, because in the case of the leading offender, France, anti-Americanism is personified in a mortal General de Gaulle, and secondly because with the expansion of transatlantic travel, and the simultaneous modernization of Europe, that continent, or the western half at least, is no longer foreign and strange to Americans. Familiarity often breeds manners more than contempt. The traveling American in Europe today is less likely to talk of Wops, Frogs, and Limeys than he was thirty years ago. But as Thai Foreign Minister Thanat Khoman remarked recently, "In Asia, we are still Gooks and Chinks to your people."

This growing disenchantment with Asia owes a good deal to war weariness over Vietnam. Other factors, however, cannot be excluded. The mass of white Americans came from Europe. Certain emotional ties, often artificially stimulated, exist between large blocs of Americans and European homelands. The same is not true of Asia.

On the contrary, the only deep American emotional involvement in Asia turned out badly. A half century ago China occupied a rather special position in American eyes. Americans were proud of their efforts to protect China from the rapacious Europeans and Japanese. The blessings of the twentieth century were being brought to China, although few paused to inquire how the Chinese themselves felt about this. The American business appetite was later whetted by Carl Crow's estimate of 400 million Chinese customers. All the tellers in Japanese banks were Chinese; the Chinese gentleman's word was as good as his bond.

When World War II came, President Roosevelt assigned to China, already riven by the struggle between Communist and Nationalists, a military and political importance she did not then deserve. A great deal of ink was spilled expanding on the "victories" won by Generalissimo Chiang Kai-shek as adumbrated by his highly efficient propaganda machine. When realists like General Vinegar Joe Stilwell attempted to provide the other, truer picture of Chinese military effectiveness they were slapped down. We were ready to suspect the British, the French, and, of course, the Russians among our allies. But the Chinese were different.

Then, of course, the Chinese Communists ran Chiang Kai-shek off the mainland and kicked us in the teeth. The American psyche has never recovered. Our national attitude toward China is built to a considerable extent on unrequited love, and this, in extension, is a formative element in the growing disenchantment with Asia generally. Why, it is asked, should we expect other Asians to act otherwise than the Chinese did?

Since the turn of the century, the dominant voice in American policy-making has been that of men and women deeply interested intellectually and emotionally in Europe, especially Western Europe. This attachment to Europe has affected this group's attitude toward Asia and its problems. When American involvement in Asia, military, political, or technological, is criticized by a Frenchman or a Dane, when a Briton or a Swede calls for an end to the American bombing in North Vietnam, they almost automatically get a hearing denied to a Thai or a South Korean or an Australian. And when an Asian leader, President Ayub Khan, for example, begins cautiously to look for other friends in hostile capitals, he is held up as an ingrate and a conspirator.

The Asians who depend on the United States have noticed this double standard and are quietly indignant about it. However, only a few, like Thanat Khoman and Paul M. C. Hasluck, Australia's capable Minister of External Affairs, have spoken out.

The most powerful argument advanced against the double

standard appeared in Mr. Hasluck's address to the twenty-second General Assembly of the United Nations. Few Americans heard him; fewer still paid attention. But Mr. Hasluck was worth listening to because he was putting his finger on a grave situation that most Americans have failed to recognize.

"Over the years," he said, "Europe taught us. We remember the lessons we learnt—respect for political independence; respect for treaty obligations; respect for territorial integrity; ideas such as that peace is indivisible, aggression has to be resisted or it will grow, the rights of small nations should be respected no less than those of the great; self-determination; the need for mutual security.

"In two World Wars that started in Europe Australia sent men across the world to fight and die in Europe for what Europe had taught us was right. But are these truths only to apply to selected regions of the world and to old-established nations? Were we right to stand up for them in Europe but wrong to stand up for them in Asia? Are they not also to be upheld among those newly independent peoples which Europe once ruled as colonies but who have now reasserted their ancient identity and who are now seeking to choose their own life and to establish it in their own territory? Does it cease to be the business of all of us when aggression takes place and freedom of choice is destroyed by force in the lands where hope of independence is newly risen? Are force, subversion, terror, and direct assaults on liberty only recognizable when they threaten a community that has settled down to the stability of a long-protected security but cannot be seen when they disturb a struggling people who are still beset by fear?

"Were we right when we answered a threat in Europe but wrong when we face a similar threat in Asia and respond to the call of a neighbor when once again the issue is the overthrow of independence by force in disregard of the will of peoples?"

Mr. Hasluck was talking, primarily, about the role of Australia and other Allies in the Vietnam war. This book is about the larger war, waged militarily, politically, and economically, that has been going on in Asia for more than a decade and whose end is out of sight. The danger to America of a new mood of isolation from Asia is that it is developing at the moment when American thought and energies should be devoted to that continent and its problems and when it should be apparent to thinking Americans in Asia that the struggle there is much wider than Vietnam. I cannot think of a single development in the United States more perilous to its future than a mass movement, now, away from Asia and its problems.

For the forces loose in Asia today, the national feuds and enmity, are of a magnitude that defy control by the Asians themselves. Even if the peoples of Asia, from Japan around to Malaysia, are finally able to form a strong political and economic grouping intended to balance the weight of Communist China, this in itself will not be sufficient. Asia cannot in its present state of development muster the strength to counter China's millions armed with nuclear weapons once they compose their internal quarrels and turn their undivided attention to the struggle between the rural and urban areas of the world. But independent Asia plus the United States can establish a deterrent power to China's ambitions.

Nor does it seem prudent that great divisive issues like Kashmir should be left to fester in the center of Asia. It is witless to say that the United States has no interest in the Kashmir dispute, that it is not involved. Any country with the global interests of the United States automatically is interested in an issue that could plunge nearly a billion people into war. And anyone who dismisses the problem with the ingenuous suggestion that it should be left to the United Nations to settle displays a startling ignorance of that organization's capacities. The United

Nations has been attempting to settle the Kashmir issue since 1947 and look how splendidly it has done!

Asia is at the boil. What happens in this vast, tumultuous continent in the next decade will affect the United States as deeply as what happened in Europe between 1910 and 1920. Throughout Asia new ideas are developing, new forces are forming, the old and the traditional are beginning to crumble.

For example, the postcolonial period is over. This means not simply that Asian economies are seeking greater independence of and greater equality with the economic giants of the West but that there is a definite shift away from the social and political forms that have continued unchanged since colonial times.

In New Delhi I protested to an Indian friend that the movement to do away with English as the national language was a mistake since English seemed to me one of the few instruments available to bind that uneasy land together.

"In the short run, yes," he said emphatically, "but in the long run, no. How can we expect to build a united India for the future on a language that only three or four per cent of the people know? Of course, we must have our own national language if only to untap the reservoir of ability and energy among the non-English speaking who are now outside the mainstream of national development. It will be the devil's own job. There will be much dislocation. But it must be done."

Politically, anticolonialism has been the most powerful element in Asia for two decades. It enjoys a certain residual influence. Witness the manner in which the Russians are able to mobilize Asian—and African—political pressure against the United States by picturing every American move in Asia as an example of "neocolonialism" or "imperialism." It is doubtful whether the sophisticated officials of the Soviet Foreign Ministry believe such stuff, but undoubtedly they realize its effectiveness.

Communism, the oldest organized political party in most of

215

Asia, benefitted enormously from anticolonialism among Asian peoples. In some cases, notably Indonesia's, the Chinese Communists went too far, too fast, in exploiting the consequent advantages. Elsewhere they have to face a new situation among the Asian masses. This is the beginning of the economic and political development of the independent nations into countries that will be resistant, if not wholly invulnerable, to Chinese Communist pressures. The great task ahead for the governments of Asia is to expedite this progress with the help of the United States and other interested countries.

"You have one great weapon against the Communists," a Singapore lawyer said. "People, young people, are beginning to reach out for the material benefits of the modern world, and I include doctors and hospitals and schools among those benefits. The Communists say that they can provide them sometime in the future but that provision depends on tearing down the present structure. You say that, if everyone puts its mind to it, the East can have them now. That is a strong argument to the young, especially the newly married."

Many Americans, deeply and naturally concerned over the war, nevertheless take a somewhat distorted view of Asia. At times they seem more willing to praise Ho Chi Minh than President Marcos. The absurd propaganda statements put out by Hanoi are given equal value with the reasoned remarks of American officials of probity and experience. When American editors can accept the statements of the National Liberation Front, that under the Communists the Vietnamese will enjoy a free press and free political institutions, there is indeed a credibility gap. Have they forgotten that the Russian Communists, moving into Eastern Europe two decades ago, promised the same sort of freedoms there? Do we have to go through another period of ingenuous acceptance of Communists' promises as fact before we learn the costly lessons of the late forties all over again?

The American dissent over the war in Vietnam is certainly understandable. What is not reasonable in it is the American tendency to underestimate, first, America's friends in Asia, and second, the basic strength of the American position in Asia.

No one who treasures freedom can quarrel with dissent, especially when it concerns a national issue as grave as the war in Vietnam. The very gravity of the issue enjoins on the dissenters the duty of self-examination. This is especially true of that segment of dissent that has reached its position through rational estimates of the arguments on both sides of the question rather than through ideological dictation.

Members of this group must ask themselves, at the outset, how much of the agitation against the United States bombing policy in Vietnam arises from a considered belief that this policy contributes only marginally to the success of American arms, and consequently is not worth the damage to American prestige, and how much is due to the inspiration of Communists, here and abroad.

One of the most striking aspects of this agitation is that it developed well before the aerial attacks on North Vietnam had become significant militarily. Since then, particularly in 1967, it attained heights of virulence in certain dissenting sectors of the population that have few parallels in our domestic affairs.

Beyond this there is another harsh question. Would the Communist world, from Peking to Havana, denounce the bombing so bitterly, demand its cessation so unremittingly, if the bombing were not effective? Of course, bombing is a propaganda ploy to be exploited. But should we not consider that the ferocity of the opposition to bombing in some sectors of dissent owes something to military considerations? We might, in this respect, take the Duke of Wellington's advice and "look on the other side of the hill" where the enemy plans his strategy.

Another question that the American dissent might consider is the identity of the true voice of Asia. It is vital in this complex situation that Americans study what is said in Hanoi by Ho Chi Minh or in neutral Cambodia by Prince Norodom Sihanouk. Premier Sato of Japan, President Marcos of the Philippines, Tunku Abdul Rahman of Malaysia, Thanat Khoman of Thailand also speak for Asia. When a country like Thailand, already beset by a Communist rebellion, decides to send an expeditionary force to Vietnam, this should be regarded as important a reflection of Asian opinion as anything said by Hanoi's rulers.

Dissent in America tends to weigh American policy and North Vietnamese policy in different scales.

On October 19, 1967 *Nhan Dan,* the official organ of the North Vietnamese Communist Party, set the price of peace: an end to the bombing of North Vietnam; recognition of the National Liberation Front, the political arm of the Viet Cong, as the representative of the South Vietnamese people; and the withdrawal of United States troops from South Vietnam.

Without laboring the point, this could be considered a formula for unconditional surrender.

Considerable weight was given to this position in discussions by dissenters who, of course, include moderates deeply concerned over their country's course as well as members of the radical left. But it was a matter of concern that less discussion was given to the approaches made by President Johnson and Secretary of State Dean Rusk to Hanoi on peace. This is not simply a question of who is right; it is that, in so desperate a situation, Americans must try to achieve objectivity.

Propaganda from the other side and America's doubts have combined to create a false picture of our position in Asia, especially in regard to Asians' attitude toward the United States. To generalize, this attitude is more hardheaded but at the same time more friendly than Americans at home understand. We are dealing here, as always, with the educated, active minority—always small in any country and very small in Asia—that runs a nation's political and economic structure, and also with the slowly growing urban and rural middle classes. Hundreds of millions of Asians, of couse, have never heard of the United States.

But the influential minority knows that Asia needs the United States. They do not subscribe to the Communist view that the Americans are in Asia to establish political hegemony leading to neocolonialism. They are more sophisticated than Americans realize. For example, they think it natural that the United States reap some profit from its presence.

"If we could do it ourselves, we'd get the nickel out of Mindanao and pocket the profits," a Manila businessman said. "But we haven't that kind of capital. And we haven't got the technical expertise. So someone else will have to do it, that is if our damned Congress will shut up, and take a profit. But the Philippines will profit, too. Anything that uses this country's resources is to our advantage in the long run."

The Asians with whom I discussed the American role in the Far East considered that the United States, in the persons of government officials, technical experts, and, surprisingly, soldiers, knew what Asia's real problems are. They were not affronted in the least by the general American feeling that the Communists must be beaten in South Vietnam and held at bay elsewhere, because that is their view, too, and many of them have spent a large part of their adult lives fighting against Communist take-overs.

They also believed that the United States, no matter how ham-handed its methods might be at times, saw the problems of Asia whole, that it was aware of the deep importance of finding food to feed hundreds of millions of more mouths in the future, that it did not expect all governments in Asia to develop faithful copies of the American democracy, that diplomats and soldiers in the last few years have shown a greater flexibility in dealing with Asians.

"You know in this country the army is in everything, selling gasoline, real estate, many other projects," a Thai official said. "At first this offended the Americans. They said it was corrupt. Of course, there is some corruption. You find it everywhere in the East. But believe me, the people get a better deal under this system than they did in the past. Your people are more tolerant. They realize that *everything* can't be the way it is in the United States. And, you know, sometimes I think they accept that our way may have something in it after all."

Finally there is agreement between Asians and Americans in Asia that the moment is urgent. There should be—but, unhappily, there is not—time for commissions to come and study the problem, for foundations to produce long, learned reports on countries and their future. The next ten years, a heart's beat in time, is the critical period. Fortunately, although this is the time for action, a great deal of the background material already has been assimilated. If Asia is changing fast, the Americans in Asia at least have an adequate knowledge of the conditions that have brought about the changes. The visitor is continually surprised at how much people like Dr. Chandler at Los Baños or Douglas Ensminger in New Delhi know about Asia. Later he learns that critics of what these men are doing, or what General Westmoreland is doing, are clearly deficient in information and understanding of Asian problems.

The United States will not be plunging into the unknown if it answers the dictates of interest and involves itself more deeply in Asia in the next ten years. No one can argue that the job of building Asia to the point where it can withstand Chinese pressure will be cheap or easy. All that can be said is that it will be cheaper or easier now than ten years hence.

There is now, there always has been, a school of thought that talks about international responsibility for Asia, meaning, in the majority of cases, the United Nations. The concept is patently ridiculous. The world organization does make an important but not a decisive contribution to Asian economic progress. But to expect it to provide the sort of political support or the amount of economic assistance necessary is to mistake the nature and capacity of the organization.

Any proposal, for instance, to the United Nations that its members join in a great cooperative effort to strengthen the governments of Southeast Asia would immediately meet the opposition of that considerable portion of the membership who are Communists themselves and who, although they might look askance at Chinese Communist penetration, would not lift a finger to prevent the weakening by Chinese pressure of governments which cooperate with the West.

A deep gulf exists between the attitude of Secretary-General Thant and that of many Asian nations on the war in Vietnam and, in addition, there are Mr. Thant's well-known differences with the United States government on the same subject. Mr. Thant's complaints about the American conduct of one of the "most barbarous" wars in history have been well ventilated. And it is right that they should be. But less attention has been paid to the very strong reservations that the Asian governments, allied in the defense of South Vietnam, have about the Secretary-General's information and judgment.

Not to put too fine a point on it, they consider that Mr. Thant is looking at the whole situation in Southeast Asia, and especially in Vietnam, from an outdated and partisan viewpoint, that of the immediate postcolonial period. Mr. Thant, they say, does not understand that the new nations are not concerned over the renewal of colonialism by the United States, but over the active military and political pressure exerted by the North Vietnamese and the Chinese Communists. They feel, too, that his stoutly held belief that a cessation of the United States bombing of North Vietnam at any time in 1966 and 1967 would have been followed by the opening of negotiations represented an ingenuous interpretation of Communist behavior. Men who had fought the Communists politically or militarily in Malaysia and Singapore and the Philippine Republic could not accept the Secretary-General's bland assurance that all the United States had to do to achieve negotiations was to surrender one of its most important weapons.

Those who suggest that the United Nations do the job in Asia forget, too, that in the economic field the world organization simply does not have the resources. In a perfect world, national governments might be willing to allow an international agency to utilize their allocations for international aid. Alas, this is not that sort of world. Effective help on a large scale for the economies of Southeast Asia comes now and will continue to come from governments pursuing their national interests. No one in the West should be horrified by this. After all, it was a government pursuing its national interest, the United States, that enabled Western Europe to recover economic stability to the point where its member states became impervious to the pressures exerted by the Soviet Union. America, too, became the central power in a military alliance, NATO, that for nearly twenty years has kept the peace in Europe. This is not the sort of example of American interest that is going to frighten the troubled governments of Southeast Asia.

The persistent idealist may suggest that at least the United Nations can "do something" about the Vietnam war. This is the sort of woolly idealism that, by exaggerating the power of the United Nations, has done so much to distort its position.

The United Nations is not a world government. To suggest that it is or is anything even remotely approaching such a government is to do the organization a grave disservice. The most reasonable assessment of the United Nations today is that it is a necessary forum for disputes among nations dominated by the two super-powers, the United States and the Soviet Union, each of which enjoys the support on essentials of its allies, clients, and satellites.

For anyone to believe that an organization so deeply divided can "do anything" about Vietnam is really incomprehensible. The United Nations is able to act effectively only when the policies of the Americans and the Russians happen to be moving along parallel lines, or when, as in the case of Korea, the Russians err and absent themselves from the Security Council, leaving the United States free to act without a Soviet veto. Because it was in the interests of both powers to halt the war between India and Pakistan in the autumn of 1965 before Peking went beyond ulti-matums to action, the Security Council was able to draft and adopt a cease-fire resolution.

The other, more recent United Nations cease-fire resolution, that which halted the Arab-Israeli war in June 1967, owes less to Soviet-American parallelism than to events on the battlefield. Had the Arab armies and air forces been lambasting the Israelis, instead of the reverse, it is most unlikely that the Russians would have joined in the call for a cease-fire. By giving instruction and arms to both regular and irregular forces on the Arab side, by providing political support for the preposterous claims of Presi-dent Nasser, and, finally, by feeding the rampant Arabs with phony information about the state of Israel's defenses, the Soviets did as much as any single power to precipitate the war. They then found that they had bet on the wrong horse. If their entry were ever to race again, he must be pulled off the track, re-turned to the stable, and trained differently. So apparently, the Russians reasoned. Consequently they voted for a cease-fire.

There is one alarming consideration arising out of the Soviet policy in the Middle East that may bear on Soviet actions in the Far East in the future.

How did it happen that so cautious a government as that presided over by Prime Minister Kosygin allowed itself to be trapped into public support for what from the outset was a lost cause fought by half-hearted armies on plans of campaign that had little relevancy to the military facts? Soviet governments since 1945, even at the height of the Cold War, always have differed from the governments of Hitler's Germany and Mussolini's Italy in their possession of a strong sense of the possible. If the Russians have lost that, we are indeed in for trouble.

As the last word on why the United Nations cannot "do something" about Vietnam, one need refer only to the advantage that the continuation of the war there gives the Soviet delegation in its dealings with a majority of the new nations of Asia and Africa and with some impressionable Europeans. As long as there are American troops in Vietnam and the war continues, the Soviets will use the situation to rally anti-American feeling within the United Nations and, indeed, throughout the world. By the sort of diplomatic gymnastics at which they are adept, the Russians can link Vietnam to the Middle East, where American support of Israel is characterized as another form of imperialism, and to southern Africa, where the United States reluctance to use force against South Africa or Rhodesia can be interpreted for the gullible as an indication that the United States, there or elsewhere, is on the side of the colonialists, the imperialists, the racists.

No, from the standpoint of global Soviet diplomacy, the American involvement in Vietnam is a good thing. As long as it remains so, the Russians will continue to seek the impossible, the withdrawal of the United States from Vietnam, to avoid substantive discussion of the issue in the United Nations, where neither North nor South Vietnam are represented, and to turn a deaf ear to entreaties that they join with the British and reconvene the Geneva Conference of 1954. The Russians naturally say they want a political solution of the war. But they have been remarkably reluctant to take any step that would facilitate that solution. Why? Clearly because they believe that, although the United States cannot be defeated in Vietnam, because of opposition at home it will never mount the sort of crushing campaign against North Vietnam of which it is capable. The Soviets are betting on war weariness in the United States to promote an indecisive peace followed by the gradual withdrawal of the American forces. From their standpoint this would be almost as valuable as a continuation of the war.

The stage would be set for the eventual take-over of South Vietnam by the Communists. The Russians, as the armorers of North Vietnam, could claim a share of the credit. The Communist Chinese, whose support has been more oral than physical, would be put in their place. The Russians, it seems reasonably certain, believe themselves in the happy position of gaining from either a continuation of the war at its present level or from an eventual American disillusionment and disengagement.

If the second power in the world is disinclined to use its influence to halt the war, either inside or outside the United Nations, little can be expected from those western countries of the second rank, great powers but not superpowers, such as Britain and France.

The British, because of their long experience in the Far East and because of the graceful manner of their departure, still enjoy considerable prestige as a people throughout the area. But no one in authority in Asia has any misconceptions about the influence of Britain on either the Soviet Union or Communist China. The British no longer have the economic or military power to provide the sort of help and support that Southeast Asia needs.

And since, in the opinion of a number of Asian leaders, including many socialists, the British Labor Party contains a large segment of conspicuously pro-Communist spokesmen with little or no knowledge of the Far East, Britain's political support in the area is suspect.

The British, at least, have acted positively in seeking to end the war mainly by imploring the Russians to join them in calling the Geneva Conference into session again. The French, whose tradition in Asia extends back almost as far as that of Britain, have acted negatively, alternately scolding the United States for intervening in Southeast Asia and proposing unrealistic settlements of the situation, all of which guarantee a position of influence for General de Gaulle.

For that reason, as well as others, his solutions command little respect in Southeast Asia. The loss of prestige and influence that France has suffered in that area—I am not talking about the common American military suspicion that French planters inform the Viet Cong of American movements in return for immunity—is the result of the General's policy in the Far East. France's recognition of Peking early in 1964 upset independent governments throughout the area, for, at a critical period in Asia's development, it could be used by the Chinese, and was so used, as proof positive of sophisticated European approval of their policies. The act of recognition brought none of the economic or diplomatic advantages to France that de Gaulle anticipated. Any western European government with relations with Peking, especially Britain's, could have told him this would be the outcome.

De Gaulle followed recognition with a series of attempts to pose as the peacemaker of the Indo-Chinese peninsula. He journeyed all the way to Cambodia to issue one of these pronunciamentos and, although it had as little effect in Southeast Asia as a tirade by a ward politician in Chicago, he returned to Paris confident that he had outlined the path to peace.

"The trouble with our French friends in all this," a South Vietnamese official said, "is that they cannot forget that they were beaten here. *Enfin,* they expect you to be beaten; they expect us to surrender to the Communists. This, to them, is rational, and to people like Couve de Murville it is more important to be rational than right."

France has lost her influence and Britain her power. Conceivably, the two countries working together might possibly exert sufficient influence on the participants in the war to move them toward negotiation. But General de Gaulle's rampant nationalism has removed any prospect of Franco-British diplomatic cooperation from the realm of possibility. Individually or collectively, there is little to be expected from Britain or France as peacemakers or as builders in Asia.

The one major power with the interest and the capacity to intervene in the affairs of Southeast Asia is Japan. Up to a point, the Japanese have everything in their favor. They are Asians. They have overcome by industry at home and generosity abroad the incubus of military defeat and foreign hostility. They are industrious, they are malleable (here Japan's change in attitude over "soft" loans is sufficient proof), and stability and prosperity in Southeast Asia—indeed, in all Asia—are of the utmost importance to Japan's export trade.

Nevertheless, the military essential is lacking. Japan, although deeply and rightly concerned over Communist China's progress in the development of nuclear weapons, is not herself in a position to offer Asia protection. She could be. She may be a decade hence. But, to strike a recurrent note, the time is now. For the next few years Japan's ultimate protection rests not in what she herself can do in the field of nuclear and conventional weapons but in the protection of the United States.

The brutal conclusion, then, is that if Asia, specifically South-

east Asia, is to be protected from Communist pressure, military
or political, to be assisted in building economic and governmental defenses against subversion, to be helped to feed itself
now and in the future, extensive United States involvement is
necessary.

There are a thousand arguments, emotional and intellectual,
against this. Beyond these is the visceral advice that it is easier
not to act, and to hope for a change in climate, than to act and
force the change. Yet it seems that none of the arguments, active
or passive, really answers the situation. We *are* involved in Asia,
from Japan to Iran. We are fond of discussing and, often, damn-
ing the reasons why we are there. But this, although a stimulating
exercise when the small hours come and the drinks dwindle, is
really irrelevant. The point is not why we are in South Vietnam
or Laos or Thailand, not why we are associated in treaty arrangements with Australia or Malaysia, but what we are going to do
about our commitments, physical and moral.

No one who has seen Asia would suggest an all-out, blanket
support of every government or every country. Support must be
selective. And once American support is committed to a country,
then, again, it must be selective. What Indonesia needs now, for
example, is not arms and other military equipment, but technological advice and the weapons of peace, bulldozers and
fertilizers, tractors and vaccines. What Thailand wants now is
military advice on how to deal with guerrillas, and political
information on where these enemies originate, who arms them,
and how, and their over-all strategy. In the Philippine Republic
the need is for straight talk, not to President Marcos and Foreign
Minister Ramos but to the landowners and industrialists who
have prospered under the protection of the United States. This,
I suggest, may be a far more important form of assistance, and
one infinitely more difficult to deliver, than some of the others
just mentioned. We are approaching a point in the Philippines

when our advice, or indeed that of anyone else, may be flouted by politicians lost in their own delusions of grandeur.

If selection is to be the rule, then, quite obviously, the initial concentration of American interest, which means the basic interest of the United States, must be in Southeast Asia. This is the critical area. If we lose in Southeast Asia, to the extent that the North Vietnamese impose their rule in South Vietnam, we must be prepared in the future, more near than distant, to encounter militant communism somewhere else in the area: Malaysia with its rubber, or Burma with its strategic position athwart the approaches to the rest of Southeast Asia, or Thailand, the rice basket of the area.

But an equal importance must be given to American interest —and interest, they tell us, never lies—in southern Asia and the great dispute between India and Pakistan over Kashmir. The state of Jammu and Kashmir is, to use words popular in England's hour of appeasement, a far-off state about which we Americans know nothing and care even less. But it is a flash point. It is the potential flash point for a war that could engulf all Asia. The reader may consider that I have emphasized this danger too often. No one who has been exposed to the fearful antagonisms of the Indians and the Pakistanis on this issue can ever doubt its danger to peace.

In this situation it is not enough in my view to help India defeat the specter of famine or to tut-tut when New Delhi buys arms from the Soviet Union or Pakistan shops in Paris or Peking for matching weapons. These two countries and their basic issue should be approached as one over-all problem. For it is as important to us to induce the Pakistanis to return to intimacy with the West, above all the United States, as it is to help the Indians control their birth rate. Selectivity should be applied here, too. But in the subcontinent, the white hot issue of Kashmir should be our first consideration. American policy should go beyond declarations in the United Nations that the issue should be settled, to active American efforts persuading both sides to settle. No American administration can retrieve the twenty wasted years of United Nations efforts in this area. What it can and should do is break fresh ground.

Certainly, we can get out of Asia. Withdraw the troops, dismantle the bases, reduce the aid programs, give no more than lip service to treaty commitments, play the wise but uninvolved counselor. The cost is small. The dividends to our self-esteem are high. This was the road that Britain took thirty years ago in Europe.

"I have watched this famous island," Winston Churchill wrote then, "descending incontinently, fecklessly, the stairway which leads to a dark gulf. It is a fine broad stairway at the beginning, but after a bit the carpet ends. A little farther on and there are only flagstones; and a little farther on still these break beneath your feet."

This is the road we will follow if we get out. And then some time, sooner or later but probably sooner, we will find that the pavement ends and that the nice, comfortable world we thought we had bought by appeasement is in fact one patrolled by tigers.

The task that beckons would be a heavy one for any people, especially the Americans, so easy-going, so fond of the good things of life, a life incomparably more comfortable than any other in the world; a people so deeply disturbed by the racial problem, that dark legacy of America's past. Yet this task is not beyond America's capacity. When one sees what Americans are doing to help Asia's development, when one encounters the cool professionalism and steady courage of the men in Vietnam, the faith is reaffirmed that there is nothing the United States cannot do when its resolution equals its energies.

The easy course is to ask Americans to ignore what is happening in Asia, especially in Southeast Asia. The simple way out, for America, is to go along with the view that what happens there is no business of ours, that we must not accept the challenge there. We are, critics of the war insist, masters of our fate. We can still choose.

Can we? We are in Asia. What we do there will decide the future of that continent in this century. If we take the wrong course now and get out, then assuredly, in ten years or less, circumstances will force our return.

This is a world we never made, and sometimes it seems as though the Americans do not understand it. With all our national pride in American achievement, we have not recognized the responsibilities that our world position forces us to bear. With all our faults, America does stand as the champion of freedom, the only country powerful enough to bring hope to those who fight for their liberty. We have to live not by the rules of the peaceful, pastoral standards of an America long past, but by those of a great power that has become deeply involved in a struggle, as much political and economic as military, for the future of unnumbered millions. They ask little: simply to live in freedom and to progress. Fate has made America their protector. Fate and death are brothers. To deny the first now is to make certain that we encounter the other soon.

Index

---

policy in Asia, objectives, 205
presence in Asia, 19, 204
relations with Pakistan, from Pakistan point of view, 147–150
suspension of arms to India and Pakistan, 134, 150
selective support to Asia, need for, 228–229
technical assistance, need for, 209
treaty with Japan, 35–36

Vasectomy, 118–119, 120
Victory, meaning of, 62
Vientiane, 11, 65, 69, 74, 79, 96, 97, 186
Viet Cong, 35, 50, 51, 52, 67, 68, 218, 226
Viet Minh, 52
Vietnam, 12, 13, 15, 16, 18, 19, 20, 35, 50, 69, 211, 214, 217, 218, 230; *see also* North Vietnam, South Vietnam
Vietnam war, 21, 27, 34, 35, 38, 61, 62, 172, 199, 214, 217, 221
Asian initiative to end, 38
characterized, 43–46, 47
concealment of equipment, lack of, 43
conflicting American opinions, effect of, 53
Village life, importance of improving conditions in, 72
Vinh, Lt. General Nguyen Van, 52

War
in Laos, 64–69
in Thailand, 64, 65, 69, 70–74
in Vietnam, connected to war in Laos and Thailand, 77
Warning by China to be heeded, 199–201
Wars of National Liberation, 14, 18, 63, 64, 84, 114, 116, 136, 137, 189, 190, 201, 205, 299
Westmoreland, General William C., 48–49, 50, 220
Wheat, new strains of, 170
White Flags, 106, 109–110
Withdrawal by U.S. from Asia
implication of, 12, 20, 63
recognition of effect of, 98
World War II, 21, 29, 55, 101

Xenophobia
of Burmese, 100, 102, 107, 113
of Chinese, 76

Yields per acre vs. increased acreage, 123

Zahir Shah, King Mohammed, 179
Zaibatsu, 25, 26